Transcend Your Boss

ZEN

and the

DIFFICULT WORKPLACE

PATRICIA G. BARNES, J.D.

Patricia G. Barnes

barnespatg@gmail.com
http://abusergoestowork.com

Paperback ISBN 978-0-9898708-0-1
E-Book: ISBN 978-0-9898708-5-6

Cover Design: Patricia G. Barnes & John Barnes-McKivigan

TABLE OF CONTENTS

Table of Contents

INTRODUCTION

All that we are is the result of what we have thought. If a man speaks or acts with an evil thought, pain follows him. If a man speaks or acts with a pure thought, happiness follows him, like a shadow that never leaves him.
                                                                –the Buddha

Being targeted for mistreatment at work is uniquely devastating. You can't just pack up and go home. You depend on your job to pay the bills. Your livelihood is at stake, and everything that flows from it. You stand to lose health and retirement benefits and face possible bankruptcy or home foreclosure. You may lose your self-identity and your standing in the community. The poor state of the economy makes it hard for many workers to find a new job, especially older workers who face pervasive age discrimination.

To make things worse, the problem of workplace abuse can be invisible to everyone but the target. Most abusers are managers who hide behind the mantle of legitimate supervisory authority to exert improper power and control over a subordinate. Abuse can go on unnoticed for months and years while the target suffers potentially devastating and cumulative mental and physical harm.

The point of Zen is to reduce human suffering.

Zen is a branch of Buddhism that focuses upon meditation. The world's first religion, Buddhism today has about 500 million adherents worldwide. Buddhism began in India and spread to China, Japan, Vietnam, Tibet and Korea and the United States. Zen evolved very differently in the West than it did in the East. North Americans tend to regard Zen as a philosophy- not a religion- that is compatible with any belief system.

Zen theory and meditation have been used by people for centuries to achieve relaxation and tranquility. Zen theory is based upon the concept of mindfulness, which is being intensely aware of the present moment. Practitioners strive for a deep sense of calm in which they can observe their thoughts and emotions in real time with detachment and objectivity.

Zen theory and tools can help any worker deal with the spectrum of difficulties encountered in a difficult workplace. This includes minor annoyances stemming from unfairness, favoritism and overwork to the most serious types of workplace abuse, including mobbing by co-workers and abuse by a manager or the employer. It's hard to imagine a scenario where mindfulness would not be of at least some help an employee.

This book is definitely *not* about using Zen to tolerate or ignore serious abuse in the workplace. A worker who does that may soon be ill and/or unemployed. If you are the target of serious workplace abuse, don't ignore it. Workplace abuse is very destructive to the health and well-being of targets. And most targets eventually are forced to leave their jobs. Some will accept a transfer but most quit or fired.

As an attorney who works in the area of discrimination and workplace abuse, I believe that Zen offers pragmatic and strategic advantages to targets. Zen can help targets stay in the game long enough to survive. It does this by helping targets respond more effectively to the abuse. Targets are better prepared to participate in an internal complaint process and see it through to a positive conclusion. Or they may gain the time needed to gather evidence to secure future unemployment compensation benefits or to wage a successful lawsuit. Or targets may have time to find a new and better job without a blot on their employment record.

Workers who are subjected to constant hostility in the workplace become worn down like rocks pummeled by ocean surf. Many targets live in a constant state of fear and dread. Overwhelming research finds that high levels of job stress lead to mood and sleep disturbances, upset stomach, headache, panic attacks, etc. Targets who are bullied for years can suffer chronic health damage. The Centers for Disease Control says evidence is accumulating that job stress plays a role in cardiovascular disease, the leading cause of death in the United States.

The stress of workplace bullying often emanates outward, like the spokes in a wheel. It can permeate all aspects of a worker's life. Some targets self-medicate with drugs and alcohol. Some bring stress home to their families, possibly leading to divorce and loss of child custody.

Zen is not a "miracle cure" for problems in the workplace but it empowers targets to exert some control over their situation. Bullies typically argue that targets are resistant to criticism or unusually sensitive. As evidence of this, they may point to an incident where the target displayed an emotional response to bullying, such as an angry retort that was overheard out of context by co-workers. Zen helps targets resist hitting the "send" button on a ill-conceived and self-destructive email to an abusive supervisor. Zen theory and tools encourage a thoughtful response to abusive behavior rather than an impulsive, self-destructive response.

Zen is about time. With enough time, a target of workplace abuse can act strategically and possibly even avoid the catastrophe of job loss. Sometimes time can make all the difference.

Workplace abuse is recognized as a form of workplace violence.

Workplace abuse sits on the same spectrum of abuse as intimate partner abuse, child abuse and elder abuse. The same patterns and power and control tactics can be seen in all of these types of abuse. Because workplace abuse generally is more accepted and less understood by society, many targets fail to discern the common patterns and tactics of abuse. They may even blame themselves. By recognizing the hallmarks of abuse, targets can avoid common pitfalls, such as self-blame, obsessive worry and doubt, anger and fear and self-isolation from friends and coworkers.

This book offers readers insight into Zen theory, instruction regarding simple mindfulness meditation techniques and diverse guided meditations designed specifically for targets of workplace abuse.

The term meditation may spur visions of a Buddhist monk sitting in the lotus position. However, meditation can be done while sitting at your chair at a desk in a busy office. You don't have to set aside an extended period of time to meditate. You can meditate on a break, for ten or twenty minutes, or for whatever time you have available. You may not achieve the Buddhist goal of oneness with the universe but you will feel calmer and better prepared to handle the challenges of a difficult workplace. The more you meditate the more benefits you will derive.

As understood in this book, Zen offers a different way of looking at life. Zen holds that most of us live in the past or future and miss our *real* life that is occurring in the present. Our thoughts about the present often are contaminated by judgments, prejudices and fears rooted in past experiences. Many targets of workplace abuse, for example, are crippled with fear of being fired, imagining all kinds of terrible consequences. This fear may prevent them from working effectively while they are still employed. Their fear is actually making it more likely they will be fired!

Zen theory holds that something which feels like a devastating blow at the time can actually be a positive development. If you are forced to leave a bad workplace, for example, you could go on to achieve tremendous success. Workplace abuse discourages innovation because workers are afraid to take chances and preoccupied with survival. The ranks of fired workers who went on to great success include Apple founder Steve Jobs, Oprah and former President Jimmy Carter. Targets of abuse may transition into a new and better job and a life that is far more fulfilling and fruitful.

This book explores Buddhist teachings passed down orally through stories and riddles. The Buddha's identity essentially was recreated after his death from the memory of his disciples. If his disciples were even close to accurate, the Buddha was an awe-inspiring figure. His simple observations and teachings were revolutionary during his time and remain so today.

I have endeavored to become acquainted with the 2,500 years of Buddhist tradition but I certainly am not an expert on this vast topic. In this respect, I follow in the footsteps of author Robert M. Pirsig who said his 1974 book, *Zen and the Art of Motorcycle Maintenance,* did not purport to accurately convey "that great body of factual information relating to orthodox Zen Buddhist practice. It's not very factual on motorcycles either."

Unlike Pirsig, I vouch for the accuracy of legal references in this book but I must add an important qualifier. The law is always changing, especially in the area of employment rights. So what is correct today may not be correct tomorrow. If you are being abused at work, you should consult an attorney who represents workers in employment cases in your state who can evaluate the law as it applies to the unique facts of your case. Nothing in this book should be construed as legal advice.

A few years ago, I took a job at an organization that specialized in family violence. I saw managers use power and control tactics on employees that were similar to those employed by abusers in cases involving intimate partner abuse. I discovered that the United States lags far behind other industrialized countries in combating workplace bullying. This led to my earlier book, *Surviving Bullies, Queen Bees & Psychopaths in the Workplace* (2012), which offers a comprehensive legal overview of the problem of workplace bullying in the United States.

I have since served as a legal consultant to targets of workplace bullying and to employers seeking to address the problem.

With respect to targets, the most devastating aspect of workplace abuse can be its emotional toll. Zen and meditation will help targets of severe bullying cope in a hostile environment but it is also a good idea to work with a licensed mental health professional.

Regarding employers, I have written many articles on my legal blog, *When the Abuser Goes to Work*, (http://abusergoestowork.com) about employers that are hit with staggering damage awards for encouraging or tolerating abusive behavior in the workplace. Only the employer can stop workplace abuse because the employer controls all aspects of the workplace. Yet, targets are not powerless. It's important to remember that the aforementioned damage awards occurred because targets had the courage to file lawsuits against these employers. As the Buddha said, all of us have the power to overcome adversity:

> Believe, meditate, see.
>
> Be harmless, be blameless.
>
> Awake to the law.
>
> And from all sorrows free yourself.

On a personal note, I extend my sincere gratitude for the guidance provided by my friend, Stephen Jacobs, a meditation expert, and to the keen eye of artist extraordinaire Paris Almond. I owe an immense debt to my copy editor and indefatigable technical advisor, John E. Barnes-McKivigan, whose patience and persistence was an inspiring example of Zen in practice.

Chapter 1

WHY ZEN?

*"A man traveling across a field
encountered a tiger. He fled, the tiger after him.
Coming to a precipice, he caught hold of
the root of a wild vine and swung himself down
over the edge. The tiger sniffed at him from
above. Trembling, the man looked down to see,
far below, another tiger waiting to eat him.*

*Two mice, one white and one black, started
to gnaw away the vine.*

*The man saw a luscious strawberry near
him. Grasping the vine with one hand, he
plucked the strawberry with the other. How
sweet it tasted!*

- the Buddha

Working in an abusive or hostile workplace is like
driving down a dark road with balding tires and no
headlights. Suddenly the brakes fail. You continue

speeding through the dark with a sense of impending doom. How can this possibly end well?

Targets of workplace abuse often don't realize what is happening until it is well into the campaign of abuse. Many targets are in denial or confused about what is occurring. When they realize that they have been targeted, they may feel a panic equivalent to that experienced by a driver whose brakes fail. Someone powerful is trying to undermine you, sabotage your work and possibly get you fired. Recent incidents that were odd or puzzling now make sense. Snubs, rolled eyes, sniggers, unfair criticism... These are all part of an orchestrated campaign.

Pictures flash through your mind. Unemployment lines – people standing around a city block in the hopes of securing a handful of low-paid jobs with no benefits. The housing foreclosure crisis is suddenly personal. What would happen if your health insurance suddenly disappeared? Sweat beads on your forehead.

All at once everything seems to be racing at warp speed, except the second hand of the clock on the wall. It takes an eternity to circle the dial.

This is where Zen comes in.

Even workers who are reasonably happy at work find Zen practices to be meaningful and enriching. Les Kaye, author of a 1996 book called *Zen at Work*, said he engaged in a meditation practice during a 30-year career at International Business Machines Corporation. According to Kaye;

"Through continued Zen meditation practice, one comes to recognize that work is a spiritual activity, not just a way to earn a living. As this recognition subtly grows and takes shape, the individual very naturally approaches work with a more giving, selfless attitude. Work becomes less stressful, more joyful and creative, more collaborative as the individual becomes more reflective and less reactive in responding to work situations."

For workers who are being abused, Zen has more urgency. It can be a lifeline. It can offer relief from fear, panic and chaos.

Zen offers a way to proceed in the face of perceived adversity with clarity and wisdom. There is no single accepted definition for Zen, which is a form of Buddhism that developed in China. This is partly because Buddhist teachings were passed down through oral story-telling rather than written documents; Westerners have picked through Zen ideologies, odd sects and obscure teachings to find what serves them best. Zen here is not about morality. It is a worldly philosophy or way of life that is compatible with any religion or no religion.

The core of the Zen philosophy is that meditation or deep contemplation allows people to better understand themselves, their interconnectedness to the universe and to reduce their suffering. Practitioners work to be in the "moment" without the filter of prejudice, opinions and pre-conceived ideas. The word

"Zen" is derived from a Sanskrit word for "meditative absorption."

Through meditation, practitioners can learn to quiet the buzzing static in their minds that prevents them from truly focusing on the present moment.

The late British philosopher Alan W. Watts said that ordinary people are in a sense asleep and Zen involves "waking up." According to Watts, "Zen is simply... that state of centeredness which is here and now."

"Reality"

A fundamental tenet of Zen is that there is no independent unconditional reality. There is the moment. The way you experience the moment depends upon your perception of what is happening. For example, you may feel like you are driving down a winding road in the darkness with no brakes. But in reality, you are sitting in your office, watching the clock. Your perception may be and often is different from reality because of your preconceived ideas about what is right and wrong, good and bad, harmful and pleasant.

Early in my career, I was a journalist who covered federal court for a daily newspaper. I got off the elevator on the third floor of the federal court building in Bridgeport, CT, and saw a distinguished looking man wearing a $1,000 suit standing in a crowd outside a courtroom. He looked at me with vibrant blue eyes and flashed a brilliant smile. I wondered if he was a big firm attorney who was representing a party in a civil case. I was shocked a few minutes later when I went into the courtroom and saw that he was the defendant in an embezzlement case involving a corporation on Connecticut's so-called Gold Coast. He was entering a plea of guilty in exchange for a reduced prison sentence. I had covered criminal trials for several years and had never seen a criminal who looked like he played tennis at a Greenwich country club. The experience freed me from my ignorance of what a criminal looks like - an ignorance that I never even knew I had.

Similarly, Zen frees individuals to see their lives with new clarity and wisdom.

The ego interprets what you see. It is the insistent voice inside one's mind that interprets reality through a filter of your past experiences. It tells you that an event makes you angry or fearful. If you eliminate the ego - or at least tone it down a bit - your perception could change. How you feel about what is occurring could change.

A *koan* is a teaching story or a riddle that is not solved by reason but by spontaneous experiential insight. Many people have heard the question, "What is the sound of one hand clapping?" It is based on a koan by Hakuin Ekaku, a Japanese Zen master who lived from 1686 to 1769, who asked his disciples: "Two hands clap and there is a sound. What is the sound of one hand?"

The following story demonstrates a Buddhist view on life's difficulties:

> *When we think we encounter a problem in life, we may blame others. We should realize the problem actually lies within us. We may not be able to change the situation but we can change how we perceive our lives. When we look at things from the view point of our ego, we cast a shadow that obscures the light of our essential self and everything seems dark. If we face the light, we can rise above our limited self-interest and can see the whole picture.*

It may be true that your boss wants to harm you. (It may not be.) Your boss may be a bully. (Or not.) But right now, at this moment, you still have your job. In fact, your suspicion that you are being bullied can give you an advantage that you didn't have before. Now you can identify the cause of the confusion that you have experienced in recent weeks. You can find out what you are up against.

A Zen theory is that people create their own suffering by worrying, being angry and feeling sorry for themselves. These emotions cause or contribute to their suffering - not the underlying problem. Conceivably, an individual could address the problem in a way that did not cause personal suffering. The more people worry, experience anger or feel self-pity, the more they suffer.

According to the Buddha: "The secret of health for both mind and body is not to mourn for the past, worry about the future, or anticipate troubles, but to live in the present moment wisely and earnestly."

Another Zen concept is that even what may feel like painful adversity actually might be the best thing that could happen to you. It is jarring and unpleasant to be under the thumb of an abusive supervisory figure who has the power to upend your life. Recognizing your situation could be very positive. This could be an opportunity for you to act constructively, deliberately and strategically to resolve a poor employment situation.

Think of a sapling in a forest, overshadowed by many larger trees. How can a sapling grow when giant

21

trees block the life-sustaining sunlight? But small trees do grow by tenaciously marshaling their strength and reaching for the light. One might even say that adversity makes a sapling grows stronger. Times of adversity can be an opportunity for an individual to develop character and to become stronger.

Options

Worrying will not help you and probably will make things worse. However, this book is not about tolerating or ignoring workplace abuse and discrimination. Workplace abuse can exact a terrible toll on a target's health. Moreover, a worker who ignores bullying may soon be unemployed. Even the Buddha acknowledged that an individual has a right to make an honest (and modest) living. Workplace bullying is widely acknowledged to be a type of workplace violence. It can be just as harmful as actual physical violence to the target and the harm can have a cumulative impact. The longer you experience it, the more damage it wreaks on your physical and mental health.

Targets of workplace abuse have many options. Under Zen theory, it would not be a solution to simply avoid the bully, as many targets attempt to do.

Zen holds that avoidance causes inner dissonance and unhappiness for the target.

Like a physical injury, a broken limb will not regain its strength if the injured person avoids using it and exercising it. Every situation is different, and there is no recommended single course of action, but it is almost always better to act rather than to ignore workplace abuse.

One solution favored in Zen circles is to respond to a bully with kindness and compassion. According to the Buddha:

> *"Conquer the angry man by love...*
>
> *Conquer the ill-natured man by goodness...*
>
> *Conquer the miser with generosity...*
>
> *Conquer the liar with truth..."*

Also, by responding with hostility, targets become hostile themselves and experience stress and turmoil.

If kindness doesn't work, the target should evaluate whether it would be useful to confront the bully and tell him/her in clear and certain terms to stop. This solution carries potential risks. The bullying could go "underground" for a while and then resume. Or, the bully could respond aggressively and retaliate against the target. Still, it might work and just doing it could make the target feel more empowered.

Targets also can explore the process of filing a formal complaint with the company's human resources department. It is often wise to first methodically collect "evidence" that demonstrates a clear pattern of abuse. Otherwise, it could be the target's word against the bully's word. The bully, often a more senior employee, would have the advantage in a contest such as this.

If a target complains and the company fails to act, the target should consider consulting with an attorney. Possibly the target has grounds to file a discrimination complaint with a federal agency. There are many other possible legal grounds depending on the circumstances, including the tort (personal injury claim) of Intentional Infliction of Emotional Distress.

The problem with almost any response to workplace bullying is that it takes time.

Time is no friend to a target of bullying.

Targets live in a state of constant worry and fear of the bullying supervisor. Workplace bullying feels like slow torture to many targets. It could literally become impossible at some point for a target to continue in a job for health reasons. That's one reason that many targets quit. They just can't take it anymore.

Using Zen tools and theories can buy targets the precious commodity of time. Zen can help targets put the bullying into perspective and overcome their anxiety and fear. Zen has been used for hundreds of years to help individuals reduce their personal anguish and suffering. You don't have to seek ultimate "enlightenment" like the Buddha to benefit from Zen.

Zen offers the possibility of maintaining a reasonably peaceful existence in a hostile environment while working toward constructive change. This is accomplished by, as the Buddha's said, "Seeing things as really they are."

Chapter 2

SUFFERING AT WORK

"Those who attempt to conquer hatred by hatred are like warriors who take weapons to overcome others who bear arms. This does not end hatred, but gives it room to grow. But, ancient wisdom has advocated a different timeless strategy to overcome hatred. This eternal wisdom is to meet hatred with non-hatred... the method of overcoming hatred through non-hatred is eternally effective. That is why that method is described as eternal wisdom." – *the Buddha*

I once worked as an editor at publishing company. I was there for less than a month when I noticed the woman in her late 50s who had the nice office across the hallway from me sobbing at her desk. Her door was open so I stopped and inquired about whether there was anything I could do. She didn't respond. The only other time I had talked to her, she said that she had moved to the state a few years earlier to care for her elderly mother. I assumed that she was disconsolate because her mother had died. After an awkward moment of silence, I went into my office and closed the door. The next day she was gone, and all of her personal possessions were gone. I later learned that she had been fired.

Suffering is epidemic in the American workplace but it goes unnoticed. It is like the tragedy depicted by the Dutch painter, Pieter Brueghel, in *The Fall of Icarus*. A boy with wax wings flies too close to the sun and falls to his death. The tragedy goes unnoticed.

Poet W.H. Auden, in the 1938 poem, *Musée des Beaux Arts*, eloquently describes the scene:

> "In Breughel's Icarus, for instance: how everything turns away
>
> Quite leisurely from the disaster; the ploughman may
>
> Have heard the splash, the forsaken cry,

> But for him it was not an important failure; the sun shone
>
> As it had to on the white legs disappearing into the green
>
> Water, and the expensive delicate ship that must have seen
>
> Something amazing, a boy falling out of the sky,
>
> Had somewhere to get to and sailed calmly on."

Millions of workers in workplaces across the country each year simply fall out of the proverbial sky and disappear. They are bullied, harassed, humiliated, cheated out of pay and benefits, made to work excessive hours, given inappropriate work assignments, unrealistic deadlines, unfairly criticized, abandoned after they are injured, etc. When the most courageous among them go to court to seek redress for the injustice they have suffered, their cases are dismissed at disproportionately high rates by federal judges. Too many people fails to see the suffering in their midst. Or they see these workers' pain as unimportant. Like the ploughman or the sailing ship in the Brueghel poem, they continue on their way.

Various surveys show that one out of every three or four workers is bullied in the United States.

In a 2011 CareerBuilder survey of U.S. workers, 27 percent said they had experienced bullying in the workplace, with the majority neither confronting nor reporting the bully. In a 2012 survey by the Society for Human Resource Management, about one-half (51%) of the organizations polled reported that there were incidents of bullying in their workplaces.

The three most common outcomes of bullying incidents reported by the organizations were decreased morale (68%), increased stress and/or depression (48%) and decreased trust among co-workers (45%).

Many targets of bullying are unfairly driven from their jobs and yet they have little or no recourse under American law.

Unlike many other industrialized countries, the U.S. government has ignored the problem of workplace bullying. However, change is afoot, largely because international corporations must follow anti-bullying laws adopted in other industrialized countries. In Europe, the Charter of Fundamental Rights of the European Union states that all workers have the right to working conditions that respect their health, safety and *dignity*. The European Union's social partnership organizations (business and labor groups that negotiate EU employment policy) signed a "framework agreement" in 2007 requiring members to implement a zero tolerance policy on status-blind workplace harassment. Why does America lag behind? There are many theories, such as American lawmakers are hostile to labor issues and courts are pro-business and anti-worker.

All of this is an argument for using Zen in the workplace. American workers need to protect themselves from workplace abuse because they can't count on our government to protect them.

Workplace Suffering is Different

Every life is filled with difficulties and obstacles that lead to suffering. As comedian Woody Allen observed: "To love is to suffer." Parents die. Children and friends move away. We all experience health problems as the "clock" winds down. One could argue that workplace suffering is the equivalent of a divorce or a death in the family.

There is a gray area between the exercise of legitimate supervisory authority and bullying. What may appear to be a proper exercise of authority can mask abuse that goes on for months or years. Workers may be defenseless to combat unfair abuse by a supervisor. It is often the accumulated impact of the abuse that is so devastating to targets.

The stakes are high with respect to workplace abuse because work is not optional for most people. They have to work to survive. Biff, a young man struggling to succeed in Arthur Miller's book, *The Death of a Salesman*, put it this way:

"It's a measly manner of existence. To get on that subway on the hot mornings in summer... To suffer fifty weeks a year for the sake of a two-week vacation, when all you really desire is to be outdoors, with your shirt off. And always to have to get ahead of the next fella. And still – that's how you build a future."

Indeed, it is the rare worker who would rather go to work than bask in the sun all day. In the current economic climate, many targets feel they have little choice but to hang on and put up with abuse. For example, older workers tend to be out of work longer than any other demographic group, and, if they are lucky enough to find a new job, it likely will pay considerably less than the old one. Eventually, the hangers-on become worn down by the abuse, blunted like the tip of a pencil. All but the heartiest are fired or forced to leave the workplace.

For some workers, a job is much more than a pay check. For many people, what they do for a living is part of their self-identity. It is integral to their very being in the world.

Abusers often target excellent workers who show initiative and creativity, work hard and are well liked.

The most gifted and productive workers may threaten a bully's self-esteem or exaggerated sense of entitlement. It is particularly devastating for these workers when they fail to succeed at a job because they have invested so much of themselves in their work.

What is Bullying?

Bullying is at the heart of workplace suffering. It is the basis for the most common types of litigation filed by employees against employers, including discrimination and sexual harassment lawsuits.

Workplace bullying is often characterized as emotional terrorism that keeps targets off balance and on edge at work.

Workplace bullying sits on a spectrum of abuse that is characterized by the improper exercise of power and control by one individual over another. Workplace bullies use many of the same tactics that are used in other types of abuse that are widely considered to be improper or illegal, including domestic violence, child and elder abuse. A bullying supervisor is not that different from a man who smacks down his partner or the swaggering child in a schoolyard who punches a smaller child to show who is boss.

In one respect, however, bullying in the workplace is different from other types of bullying. It is characterized by a power imbalance that often makes the problem invisible and intractable. The American legal system accords employers and their agents extraordinary power over employees and it is not difficult for a supervisor to misuse that power. In the United States, a worker who lacks a contract or who is not covered under a union agreement can be fired by an employer "at will" or for any reason – as long as it is not an illegal reason (e.g., discriminatory). There are exceptions to this "at will" rule but they are difficult to satisfy and fail to protect most workers who are fired.

Occasionally, a worker is targeted by a co-worker who recruits others in a campaign of harassment against the target. This is called "mobbing," a term derived from the natural world, where a member of one species is attacked and driven out by others because it is considered different or seen as threatening in some way.

General definition of workplace bullying:

1. Harassing, offending, socially excluding someone or negatively affecting his/her work tasks.

2. The interaction or process occurs repeatedly and regularly and over a period of time.

3. The process escalates until the subordinate is left in an inferior position, demoted, fired or forced to quit.

Jane (not her real name) was disconsolate after learning that she had submitted a report to her boss that contained an embarrassing error. Instead of "it's" the word was spelled "tit's." The mistake garnered many guffaws throughout the office. Any worker would be embarrassed by such a mistake but Jane was distraught. The spell checker hadn't caught it. She didn't catch it. Jane's boss had angrily confronted Jane, demanding an explanation.

One thought kept replaying over and over again in Jane's mind: "How could I have been so stupid?"

There were many reasons for Jane's mistake and being stupid was not one of them. Jane's supervisor micro-managed Jane's schedule and work assignments, often leaving Jane upset, frustrated and defensive. Earlier in the week, Jane arrived at her desk a few minutes late. Furious, her supervisor told Jane that she would receive a warning the next time she was not sitting at her desk and ready to start work at the stroke of 8 a.m. Jane was shocked. "I'm never late," she protested. "I stopped in the rest room because I spilled coffee on my shirt. Are you telling me I can't stop at the rest room if I need to?"

The next day, the supervisor gave Jane a substantial project that was due on Friday. Exasperated,

Jane said she had several other assignments with imminent due dates. "Your workload is no heavier than anyone else's," the supervisor insisted. "In fact, you have less on your plate." Her supervisor rolled her eyes and asked, "Do you want me to help you establish a work plan?"

Working frantically, Jane managed to meet the deadline but she didn't have enough time to proofread her work as carefully as she normally would have.

At her next employment review, Jane's boss cited her "egregious mistake" as evidence of the over-all poor quality of Jane's work. When Jane tried to defend herself, she was called "resistant" to criticism and warned that her failure to improve could result in termination. Jane filed an 11-page response to the poor performance review with the Office of Human Resources but never received a reply.

Shortly thereafter, Jane attempted to transfer to another department, for a job that was similar to her current position. She was not selected for hire. She began to apply to every employer in the region who had a potential job for which she was qualified but she got no nibbles.

Within a few months, Jane, a 47-year-old single mother of two teenagers, had exhausted her sick leave with a variety of stress-related illnesses. Meanwhile, her boss had shifted some of Jane's important work responsibilities to others, leaving Jane feeling humiliated, spending her time on inconsequential and menial tasks. Jane received a formal warning for being seven minutes late to work after she got stuck in traffic after dropping her daughter off at school. She knew that she could be fired if she received just one more warning.

Jane arrived at work one morning, sat down at her desk and turned on her computer. Suddenly she felt a shortness of breath and heart palpitations. She was alarmed and panicked. "I just knew that if I didn't quit right then and there I would have a nervous breakdown," she said.

Many workers do not realize that they are targets of workplace bullying and abuse. Like Jane, they blame themselves for mistakes or shortcomings. Other targets endure months of bullying before they finally figure out what is going on.

By then, the bully has had time to destroy the target's reputation and create a paper trail that leads inexorably to the target's ouster.

Some targets suspect what is going on is bullying but are fearful that if they complain they will not be believed or will be subjected to retaliation. Human resources officers traditionally have ignored bullying complaints or sided with the bully. (Ironically, research shows that a quarter of HR officers report being targets of bullying themselves.)

Common tactics used by bullying supervisors

- Hostile verbal behaviors, shouting and belittling.
- Sabotaging the target's work.

40

- Providing insufficient information to complete a task.
- Imposing unrealistic deadlines.
- Blaming the target for things over which the target had no control.
- Isolating the target by disparaging the target to other managers and signalling to the target's co-workers that the target is "trouble."
- Insisting the bully's way is the only right way.
- Removing responsibilities and assigning the target trivial tasks.
- Micromanaging.

After Jane left her job, her former supervisor began bullying Jane's successor, a young woman who had no concern that she could find another job. She immediately complained to senior management. The supervisor was ordered to complete a two-hour on-line management training program. Sparks continued to fly. The company then conducted a 360 degree "environmental survey" of individuals in the department. The company learned that the supervisor was widely considered to be an angry and impatient control freak. Shortly thereafter, the supervisor announced she was leaving the company because she had found another job.

Meanwhile, the company lost a valuable employee, Jane, and was forced to hire and train Jane's successor. The company incurred additional expenses in lost work time, lower productivity and higher medical costs. The company's reputation suffered – Jane, her friends and family bad-mouth the company at every opportunity.

The abuse Jane suffered also affected her co-workers, some of whom began to circulate *their* resumes. Research shows that employees who witness a co-worker being bullied often duck for cover so they won't be singled out and then start looking for another job.

Who's Fault?

When confronted, an abusive supervisor often tries to make it appear that the target is neurotic, paranoid or overly emotional.

> *Bullies often characterize their abuse as "tough management" or adherence to "high expectations."*

Some observers say that abusive managers frequently are unaware of the impact of their actions upon co-workers and subordinates. An executive coach argues that many of her clients are shocked when they are told that a bullying complaint was lodged against them. She says these managers often are poorly trained or simply lack the ability to manage their psychological stressors and "end up venting their distress on those around them."

I am more inclined to side with Robert Fulghum, author of the 1986 bestseller, *All I Really Need to Know I Learned in Kindergarten.* We all know that we should "play fair," "don't hit people," "don't take things that aren't yours," and "say you're sorry when you hurt somebody." I am skeptical that most bullying managers lack awareness of the harm they inflict upon others but I also think this is not the real issue - employers have a legal and moral responsibility to train and monitor managers to insure a bully-free workplace. The employer must insure that managers do not abuse and mistreat subordinates.

At the extreme end of the bullying spectrum, are psychopaths. They enjoy making their subordinates miserable. Several books have been written in recent years describing the rate of psychopathy among corporate managers. Psychopathy is a personality or mental disorder characterized partly by antisocial behavior, a diminished capacity for remorse, and poor behavioral controls. A 2005 study by researchers in England compared a group of business managers with a group of hospitalized criminals (including psychopaths) and found the business managers were more likely to have psychopathic qualities.

About one percent of workplace bullies are actual psychopaths; up to 15 percent have psychopathic tendencies.

Do most bullies know exactly what they are doing or are they clueless? There is no definitive answer to this question. It would not be surprising if a psychologist or a business coach had a different perspective than a target or an attorney who represents bullied workers. Like everything else, the answer is probably a mixed bag.

Bad Company

Of course, not all bullies are individuals. The problem is much more complicated, troubling, and insidious. In fact, it is deeply entrenched in our legal system, which largely places the onus on employees to protect their rights.

Unethical employers often use workplace abuse as a tool for strategic and pragmatic reasons. For example, many lawsuits have been filed against employers who began bullying workers after they complained that they were not paid all of their wages or overtime. The Progressive States Network in 2012 estimated that more than 60 percent of low-wage workers suffer wage violations each week, losing an average of $51 a week or $2,634 per year. Many workers are afraid to complain because they fear- quite legitimately -that doing so will make them appear to be a "troublemaker" in the eyes of management and they will be driven out of the workplace.

Unethical employers may target good workers for abusive treatment to avoid other legal obligations. For example, a lawsuit was filed by a factory worker who was fired after he told his boss that he had fallen on the factory floor. His boss feared the worker might file a worker's compensation claim. Another lawsuit involved an employer who wanted to downsize without paying unemployment benefits. That employer intentionally made working conditions a living hell for good workers because they were no longer needed.

Employers count on the fact that most workers either do not know their rights or cannot afford to take the necessary legal steps to protect their rights.

Employers know that many workers lack the resources to file a lawsuit and the few cases that do make it to court likely will be summarily dismissed by judges who are unsympathetic to workers' rights.

There is no federal or state law at present to prevent employers from subjecting employees to what in other contexts would be considered a "hostile workplace" *unless* the abuse is directly tied to illegal discrimination. Technically, the U.S. Occupational Safety and Health Act requires employers to provide workers with safe working conditions but, with some minor exceptions, the law is not enforced with respect to workplace bullying. In reality, the law is not well suited to the problem of workplace bullying because it contains no private cause of action and the penalties available are very modest fines.

The bottom line is that employers in the United States have little incentive to address the problem of workplace abuse.

Yet, only employers can address the problem of workplace abuse. Employers control all aspects of the workplace, including management's level of tolerance for abuse. If the employer refuses to tolerate abusive management, it stops.

In many other countries, employers have an obligation to prevent bullying by providing appropriate anti-bully training to supervisory personnel and supervising managers to insure compliance with company policies. In France, severe sexual harassment is a criminal offense that carries up to three years in prison. In the United States, by contrast, it is very difficult to hold employers accountable for bullying, sexual harassment and discrimination.

Violations of employee rights in America are civil in nature. The onus is on the employee to seek damages after his/her rights have been infringed. Yet, most Americans effectively lack access to justice because of the high cost of hiring an attorney and the lack of legal assistance due to federal government cut backs in funding civil legal assistance to the poor.

One of the positive features of Zen theory is that it empowers individuals to help themselves.

Sadly, employees who are targeted for abuse may have no one but themselves to fall back on. It is not realistic to expect a superhero to be waiting in the wings to help. In fact, it's not realistic to expect Human Resources to help; HR represents management's interests, not yours. Workplace abuse can be a very lonely experience for targets. Targets often isolate themselves, abusers isolate targets, and co-workers may avoid targets out of fear that they are "persona non grata."

Zen uses the tool of meditation whereby individuals engage in deep contemplation to relieve stress and gain clarity about what is happening in their lives.

Chapter 3

WHAT THE BUDDHA KNEW

"To conquer oneself is a greater task than conquering others." -*the Buddha*

The Buddha knew something about suffering.

Prince Siddhartha Gautama was born about 2,500 years ago into royalty at Kapilavastu, which lay in the foothills of the Himalayas near the present day Nepalese-Indian border. He is thought to have lived 500 years before the birth of Jesus Christ. According to lore, his mother, Queen Maya, had a dream before he was born in which a white elephant with six tusks entered the right side of her body and disappeared. An astrologer predicted that she would give birth to a son who would either be a great political leader who would conquer the world or an enlightened religious being.

Prince Gautama's father, King Suddhodana, wanted his son to be a great warrior. The king thought he could insure this by creating a life for his son that was so comfortable and insulated from the harsh realities of life that he would never want to leave. The prince lived in an opulent palace with the finest food, clothing and entertainment. And every time a flower began to wilt, it was removed before Prince Gautama could see it.

At the age of 16, however, Prince Gautama persuaded his attendant, Channa, to take him outside the palace on a series of excursions.

During the first trip outside the palace, the prince saw an old man with shriveled skin who was bent over and leaning on a walking staff. He asked Channa what was wrong with the man and Channa replied, "He's old. Everyone who lives for a long time gets old and looks like that."

On the second trip, Prince Gautama saw a man who was delirious with fever and whose skin was covered with blotches. "He is sick. Everyone is subject to disease," said Channa.

Prince Gautama, on the third trip, saw a corpse lying on the side of the road. Channa told him the man is dead, adding, "We all die, sweet prince."

Finally, on the last excursion, the prince saw a holy man dressed in rags seated cross-legged under a tree, looking calm and peaceful. "What sort of man is this?" asked the prince. Channa told him the man "is a homeless wanderer in search of truth."

Prince Gautama was shocked by the suffering he had seen and asked himself, "How can I enjoy a life of pleasure when there is so much suffering in the world?" At that point, Prince Gautama's destiny revealed itself to him and he vowed to one day follow the holy man's example.

At the age of 29, Prince Gautama, now happily married and the father of a son, renounced his privileged life, cut his long hair, and set out on a spiritual journey to find out how to end humanity's suffering. "Nothing is stable on earth," he said, "Nothing is real. Life is like the spark produced by the friction of wood. It is lighted and is extinguished – we know not whence it came or whither it goes... There must be some supreme intelligence where we could find rest. If I attained it, I could bring light to man. If I were free myself, I could deliver the world."

For six years he wandered in the jungle as a poor monk, studying and living as an ascetic, enduring extreme deprivation and near starvation. But he did not find the answers he sought. He abandoned the path of "self-mortification" for a more moderate approach to seek the truth that he called the middle way.

Enlightenment

In the year 528 B.C., Prince Gautama, then 35, sat down under the Bodhi tree (Bodhi means "awakenment" or "enlightenment") in the *asana* position (with raised knees and upturned palms) and declared that he would not leave until he found an end to suffering. Prince Gautama was visited in the night by

Mara, the Lord of desire, and armies of evil spirits who all tried to divert him from his virtuous path. Using self-discipline, he resisted these temptations and remained absorbed in concentration. At the first glimpse of the morning star, he experienced his awakening. He achieved "nirvana" or "enlightenment" - which is described as a perfect state of being where the self achieves a oneness with the universe. He became the Buddha, a term that means "to wake up."

The Buddha realized that all things are impermanent – nothing stays the same. Because the world is constantly changing there is no "self." And there is nothing that human beings can cling to that will give them any sense of enduring happiness.

He concluded that the world is a painful place marked by unending suffering.

The Buddha taught that deep compassion, loving kindness, mindfulness and detachment from negativity are the keys to overcoming human suffering. With enlightenment, his fears of the future, greed, hatred and delusions melted away. When there was no longer a false concept of selfhood, there was no self left to die and the Buddha could see the world with perfect clarity.

Finally, with his enlightenment, the Buddha's soul was liberated from the endless cycle of suffering in life, death and rebirth. A traditional Buddhist belief is that the soul is reborn consecutively in different bodies and different places until it reaches enlightenment.

Jean Smith, in *The Beginner's Guide to Zen Buddhism*, describes enlightenment as "the state of being where there is no grasping, no desire for things to be different from the way they are..."

One ancient story compares enlightenment to the clarity of a mountain recess. There is a mountain lake where the water is clear and undisturbed. A person with good sight stands on the bank of the lake and watches the shells, gravel, pebbles, and the fish swimming and resting. Individuals who achieve true insight can see what is really going on in their life. Their minds are clear. Nothing disturbs them.

Enlightenment occurs when people have absolute clarity about what is going on in their lives.

For the next 45 years, the Buddha travelled throughout India garnering disciples and teaching the "dharma" (the law of the cause of suffering and the path to its cessation). The Buddha did not claim to be a god and said he was not even the first Buddha. He taught that "[a]ll living beings have the Buddha nature and can become Buddhas."

The Buddha was surprisingly progressive and open-minded for his era. He rejected prevailing Hindu doctrines, animal sacrifices, wars, violence, killing, slavery, the caste system, discrimination and inequality of men and women. At the time, the caste system was believed to deny salvation to millions of Indians.

Four Noble Truths

Among the most important of Buddha's teachings are the Four Noble Truths. These truths are:

1) Birth, decay, sickness, death and desire cause all people to suffer.

2) Suffering is caused by desire to control one's life and environment, and by clinging to the notion of self.

3) There is a way to end suffering. It is by eliminating its cause or ceasing to engage in desire and ego.

4) Suffering can be ended by following the Noble Eightfold Path, which involves a set of resolutions characterized by a concern for morality, concentration, moderation, positive action, and wisdom.

Noble Eightfold Path

Zen does not require that anyone follow a specific moral code. Zen has developed in the West as a non-religious philosophy to help people reduce suffering. The Buddha, however, taught his disciples to follow a specific moral code called the "Eightfold Path." Many aspects of this path are common in Western religious beliefs.

The Eightfold Path consists of:

1) Right understanding (Buddhist orthodoxy).

2) Right thought (positive, logical).

3) Right speech (truthful, non-hateful).

4) Right action (honesty).

5) Right livelihood (do no harm).

6) Right obedience (lawful life).

7) Right mindfulness and

8) Right meditation.

The Buddha's teachings represent the Middle Way" because they occupy the middle position between the extremes of complete denial of pleasure and self indulgence. Generally, Buddhists must abstain from taking of life, stealing, sexual misconduct, lying and intoxication.

The Buddha believed that it is in the nature of human beings to suffer from greed, jealousy, envy and negativity. He observed that the things people want the most often cause them the most suffering. The Buddha said people should have adequate food, shelter, and clothing but he taught that a life consumed with greed and materialism ultimately will leave people empty and unfulfilled.

The Buddha passed away around 486 BC at the age of eighty. He is said to have died of food poisoning after his host served him bad pork.

His last words were: "All individual things pass away. Strive on, untiringly."

In this statement, he admonishes his followers to refrain from holding anything as worth grasping at or clinging to. He urges them to refrain from mindlessly attach to anything.

After he left the world, the Buddha's teachings (called sutras) spread from India into Sri Lanka, Central and Southeast Asia, Tibet, China, Korea, Japan, and in the 20th century, to Europe and the Americas. Buddhism evolved with countless sects, schools and belief systems. The oldest surviving form of Buddhism today is called Theravada (which means "The Teachings of the Elders") Buddhism and flourishes in Southeast Asia and Sri Lanka.

The Buddha set in motion a fundamental shift in the way we think about human suffering and salvation. The Buddha empowered individuals to take responsibility for themselves rather than wait for a deity to intervene or to suffer and wait for the promise of an after-life. In his book, *Buddhism and Modern Thought*, author E. G. Taylor writes: "Buddhism is the earliest ethical system where man is called upon to have himself governed by himself." Buddha continues to embody the spirit of kindness, compassion and the hope for relief of suffering.

Like the Buddha, targets of workplace abuse know the meaning of suffering. They toil in a climate of hostility and abuse, often trapped by a bad economy and the need for a paycheck. Thanks to the Buddha, however, targets don't have to journey into the wilds for six years and sit under a Bodhi tree to find the answer to their suffering. What would the Buddha do? The Buddha advocated the using meditation to calm the anguished mind and find clarity and peace.

The following chapters will show that anyone can meditate, at any time of the day or night. This is a simple exercise- a form of intense concentration- that truly can make a transforming difference in a hostile workplace. Meditation can make a difficult workplace more bearable and less injurious to the spirit.

The practice of meditation may even help targets hang on long enough to work their way through the employer's internal complaint process so they can salvage their job or find another solution to the bullying.

Chapter 4

WHAT IS REAL

I have realized that

the past and the future

are real illusions,

that they exist only in the present,

which is what there is and all that there is

— Alan Watts

It is a Zen concept that people live in a state akin to self-delusion. They live with craving, desire, pride, anger and hate. They lack essential self-awareness. For example, many people think that material possessions will bring them happiness. They work frantically to gain more and more possessions only to be disappointed. The Buddha, among others, teaches that real happiness comes from love and compassion. Zen involves recognizing and letting go of delusions and negative mental properties, which are known as "defilements." When all of these defilements are gone, what remains is inner peace.

It is always useful for workers who fear they are being targeted by a bully to engage in a process of self-reflection.

Many of us bring baggage into the workplace that can negatively influence our perception of people and events.

Some of us have unrealistic expectations about the job. Some workers expect they are entitled to constant praise and that they will never be criticized. Such expectations make unhappiness at work inevitable.

There is a well known Zen story about a woman whose first-born son had died. She was grief stricken and roamed the streets carrying the dead body. A kind man took her to the Buddha and she asked him if he could bring her son back to life. The Buddha said he could bring the boy back to life if she brought him a handful of mustard seeds. Then, he said, "But the seeds must come from a family that has not known death." She went throughout the village, from house to house, asking for mustard seeds. At each house, she was told, "I lost my father last year," "I lost my baby too," "My sister died," "I lost my husband," etc. She could not find a single household that had not been visited by death.

She returned to the Buddha and said, "Now I understand your teaching. Everyone will die. No family is spared from death." The Buddha said, "No one can escape death and unhappiness. If people expect only happiness in life, they will be disappointed."

No job will be enjoyable all of the time. There will be days when your boss is out of sorts and grouchy or a co-worker says something insensitive or even hurtful. There will be days when your hard word and dedication are not acknowledged or appreciated. To paraphrase the Buddha, if people only expect happiness at work, they will be disappointed. Workers who are worried they have become a target of workplace abuse should first assess whether they are overreacting to what in reality are just run-of-the-mill slights and petty grievances.

No Fan of Authority?

Usually when a target feels that he or she is being bullied, it is with good reason. But not always. Employees who are concerned that they are being targeted should contemplate whether they are, in fact, being bullied. Or is it a question of perception?

According to the Buddha, a boss and a worker each have obligations toward each other. The Buddha taught that a boss should assign work that is suited to the employee's abilities, pay decent wages, care for workers when they are ill, and refrain from overworking them. In return, the Buddha said, workers should take only what they are given, work hard, and defend their employer's good name. Are you fulfilling your part of the bargain with your employer?

Zen theory posits that the ego can be a formidable barrier to seeing things the way they really are. For example, if you tend to resent authority figures, you may experience any display of authority as being aggressive or hostile. You may react defensively. A boss who lacks emotional intelligence may inadvertently fan the flames of your discontent. Soon both of you will be engaged in conflict.

One Zen story uses the metaphor of light and shadow to provide insight into self-reflection:

> "When we experience a problem in life, we should realize that the problem actually lies within us. We may not be able to transform the situation, but we can transform ourselves and how we perceive our lives. When we look at things from the viewpoint of our separate ego-self, we cast a shadow that obscures the light of our essential self and everything seems dark. If we turn and face the light, we rise above our limited self-interest and can see the whole picture."

Those of us who have not reached the state of pure enlightenment often have difficulty rising above our limited self-interests. Still, it is worth making the effort to try. Observe how you interact with your boss and other authority figures in the workplace. Is there anything you can do to improve your relationships with your supervisor? If it is appropriate, talk to others who work or have worked for your boss and ask them about their experiences, how they feel about the boss and how they get along with their boss.

What is Your Nature?

The Dalai Lama, in his book, *The Art of Happiness in the Workplace*, observes that one's emotional make-up and attitudes are important for happiness in the workplace.

"For example," he writes, "if someone gets a job and if the person has a sense of inner contentment and also is not greedy, to that individual that work may be very fulfilling. On the other hand, there may be a second individual who has the same job but that individual may be much more ambitious and thinks that he deserves a better job than this and this work is too demeaning. He's jealous of other colleagues. Then the same work may not give a sense of fulfillment..."

Think also about your personal history in the workplace. Is this the first time you have reported to a bullying supervisor or do you always work for abusive bosses? If it is the latter, you may be inadvertently contributing to the problem. If you do not address this situation, you are dooming yourself to an endless circle of tumult, anxiety and suffering in the workplace. You can stop the destructive pattern by working with a good therapist to identify what has occurred in your life that results in your finding yourself repeatedly in this difficult situation.

We all know people who seem to have a "problem" with authority. In fact, I suspect we all do to some extent. Matt Groening has done a great job exploring the underlying tension between management and labor on the popular animated television show, *The Simpsons*. Mr. Burns, Homer's boss at the nuclear power plant, is greedy and completely lacking in empathy for his employees. Burns' catchphrase is, "Release the hounds!" Burns also owns the Montgomery Burns

Institute for Soul Extraction next to the hospital. Is it more likely that Mr. Groening would thrive in a corporate office on the 6th floor of the General Electric Building or sitting behind a drafting table in his home office?

Some people are better suited to work in a gray suit at a fancy office in a gleaming skyscraper. Some people are better suited to work in blue jeans, outdoors, as a farmer or a park ranger. Does your workplace fit your personality?

Or maybe it is an institutional problem? The working environment is very different for corporate employees at the Gothic-inspired General Electric Building than it is for workers at the Googleplex "campus" at Mountain View, CA. Both types of employees are expected to work hard but Google workers are more independent and come and go as they please. And the Google campus features 18 cafeterias with diverse menus, multiple sand volleyball courts, replicas of SpaceShipOne and a dinosaur skeleton. On the other hand, while Google workers may not work a 9-to-5 schedule, they are expected to work notoriously long hours.

The bottom line is that all workers need to reflect upon their nature and to find the workplace and working environment that best suits them. Hanshan, a Buddhist poet from China, opined centuries ago that there were too many intellectuals in the world "who've studied far and wide, and know a lot of things. But they don't know their own original true nature and thus are wandering far from the Way."

I worked at a non-profit organization which insisted its employees use an In/Out Board to indicate when they left the building. Management changes occurred after I was hired but before I started work and, much to my dismay the boss assigned to supervise me was a micromanager and critic. She was a rigid clock-watcher with no sense of humor. She had not attended any of my interviews for the position and probably would not have hired me if she had. During my interview, I made it a point to tell managers that I did not like to work in an environment where employees are "micromanaged."

The In/Out Board had a lever that moved to the left or right to indicate whether you were in or out. There was a space and a marker so that you could write the time of your departure and return. Every afternoon I left my office, with its hermetically sealed windows, and passed by the In/Out Board without stopping. Often, I ran across the street and bought a cup of coffee to bring back to work to drink at my desk. I would occasionally find myself thinking negative thoughts:

"I'm a professional not a toddler in a nursery school."

"I worked 20 hours of overtime last month for which I received no pay because I'm supposedly an exempt professional employee – but they're monitoring my coffee break?"

"It's not like I am an emergency room doctor who might have to save a life. The closest thing to excitement around here is a fire drill. I work on a computer all day ... which is why I need some coffee."

As I walked to and from the office, it would sometimes occur to me that I might run into my supervisor and be "caught" outside the building without a pass. I felt like a high school student playing hooky. Thus, I couldn't fully relax on my measly 10-minute afternoon break.

One day I sat in my office and pondered my unhappy situation. Management had misrepresented the culture of the organization. The person whom I was told would be my boss was switched at the last minute for someone with no management experience, far less substantive experience and a dour personality. Had I known, I never would have moved across country with my child to work for this boss or this employer.

The real purpose of the In/Out Board was to discourage employees from taking breaks. Maybe that's why I never saw another co-worker at the coffee shop. But why did I resist using the In/Out Board when I could see that it was impairing my ability to relax on my breaks? Who was I penalizing except myself? I realized that it would take less energy to use the In/Out Board than it was taking me to feel resentful and unhappy every day. If my boss had the temerity to confront me about taking a lousy mid-afternoon coffee break, I would stand up for myself and demand to be treated like a professional.

Looking back, I realize I was naive to rely solely upon the representations of managers at my interview. I should have asked to speak separately to rank-and-file employees so that I could learn about the true nature of the organization. In my excitement about the possibilities of a new job, I didn't exercise sufficient "due diligence" to protect myself and my family. I had learned a painful lesson but I hope the experience will ultimately prove to be valuable. I will never make *that* mistake again.

Is it Bullying?

Workplace abuse is not about perceived slights and wounded feelings. It is a repeated and intentional pattern of behavior by someone who usually wields greater power. Bullies can hide in plain site in the American workplace, where abusive treatment literally is considered a prerogative of management. One way to tell whether you are being bullied is to look for the patterns.

Many of the behaviors seen in other types of abuse are evident in workplace bullying. These include demeaning comments, being overly critical, unrealistic deadlines, withholding information required for a task, isolating the target, etc. In one case, a supervisor actually turned off a calendar alert system on her subordinate's computer so she would be late to departmental meetings.

Abusers tend to be adept at subtly manipulating circumstances to enhance their stature while diminishing the target's. Their management style is often referred to as "Kiss Up and Kick Down." They rarely miss an opportunity to disparage the target, especially when the target is not present. They may criticize the target in management meetings and discourage other managers from inviting the target to participate in team projects. Some targets say the manager who bullied them acted with the strategic skill of a master chess player; each move was calculated to checkmate the target.

Still, it is not bullying when a supervisor tells a subordinate employee to perform an appropriate job-related task. It is management's role to implement an appropriate work plan that will accomplish the legal goals of the organization. Managers delegate work among subordinate employees. Even in organizations that emphasize teamwork, the team reports to someone. Yet all workers have an inherent right to be treated with dignity and respect. Workers may be subordinates but they are not serfs, indentured servants or slaves.

Civility in the workplace, or the lack thereof, can be in the eye of the beholder. Is it disrespectful when a supervisor issues an order without a polite qualifier? It depends on who you ask. A busy chef in a commercial kitchen would say there is no time for pleasantries and none are expected. But people who work in small offices expect courtesies that are common in interpersonal relationship. And customers who patronize service providers also have expectations. I went to a dentist once who barked at his assistant and I immediately changed dentists.

There is an on-going debate about what is and is not disrespectful in a workplace.

The answer to the question of what level of civility is required in a workplace is continually changing. Today, it would be unthinkable for a supervisor to physically push or strike an employee but this was not uncommon a hundred years ago. Also, it is difficult to define a concept like "respect" expansively enough to include the universe of factors that should be included and excluded. To some extent, the debate over workplace civility evokes U.S. Supreme Court Justice Potter Stewart's comment about obscenity, "I know it when I see it."

There is no law against workplace bullying in the United States but the U.S. Supreme Court has provided guidance on what it considers to be a "hostile" workplace or work environment in the context of federal civil rights laws. Title VII of the Civil Rights Act of 1964 makes it illegal to subject a worker to a hostile work environment because of discrimination based upon certain protected characteristics (e.g., race, sex, religion, etc.)

According to the U.S. Supreme Court:

> *A hostile work environment occurs when unwelcome conduct is so severe and pervasive that it interferes with the target's work performance or creates a work atmosphere that is offensive or abusive.*

The Court has ruled that a single instance or utterance that is offensive generally is not considered to be sufficiently egregious to affect the conditions of employment enough to violate Title VII.

Advocates of workplace anti-bullying legislation question why anyone should be subjected to a hostile workplace and propose that all workers– even those who are not members of a protected class– be entitled to the same protection and remedies of Title VII.

Clueless Boss?

Stephanie, an administrative assistant, could hear her boss speaking in his office with his door closed. He was arguing on the telephone with his ex-wife about visitation with his three young children. He used vulgar, sexist language and then slammed the phone down on the receiver. After a few minutes of silence, his door burst open and he emerged red faced.

"Are you a total incompetent? I told you I wanted the Foster file."

He slammed a folder on her desk with such velocity that she felt a swish of wind on her face. He stooped and brought his face close to hers and hissed, "If you can't do your fucking job then I'll find someone who can!" He turned and went back into his office, slamming the door.

After the shock wore off, Stephanie (not her real name) realized she was shaking uncontrollably. She felt like the victim of a hit-and-run emotional assault. She collected her purse and went to a restroom, where she cried in a bathroom stall.

Standing alone, the behavior of Stephanie's boss may not fit the classic pattern of bullying. It is unlikely that Stephanie could prove a "hostile work environment" based upon this single incident. Arguably, he did not intend to harm Stephanie, though she was harmed by his behavior. She was more like an innocent bystander hit by a stray bullet. Yet, her boss' behavior was completely unacceptable and it is not a valid excuse that he was acting under the stress of a difficult divorce.

A long-time career counselor contends that most bullying bosses fundamentally are clueless managers. They cannot deal with the stress they are experiencing or they were never trained in proper management techniques. But Stephanie should not tolerate the kind of behavior displayed by her boss, and neither would a wise employer. Stephanie should research her company's complaint policy and lodge a complaint A wise employer would hold her boss accountable and ensure that the bullying stops then and there.

Employers have a broad array of tools to use to discourage bullying behaviors, including coaching, training, anger management or disciplinary action. An employer who has notice of bullying and fails to act is inviting a host of unnecessary problems, from needless turnover to a costly lawsuit.

Fear of the Future?

Many targets are paralyzed with fear about what might happen in the future. Targets fear retaliation, not being believed, of being labeled overly-sensitive. They especially worry about being fired. When the bully is a supervisor, the target concludes (often correctly) that the bully is seen as having more value to the organization. Or perhaps the target thinks the bully has friends in senior management who will take the bully's side. Targets worry, often justifiably, that they won't get a fair shake. Yet, failing to tell management that you are being bullied could be a serious mistake.

A bullying complaint triggers an important legal duty for the employer, and important legal protections for the target. Once the employer has notice of bullying, the employer must act or risk significant liability down the road. And, importantly, the employer must insure that the target is not subject to retaliation. If you don't complain, the bullying will almost certainly continue and could wreak havoc on your mental and physical health.

One of the most important issues with respect to a complaint should be its timing – when is the optimal time to file a complaint. Unless a bullying instance is particularly serious, you should consider waiting until you have collected enough evidence to demonstrate a pattern of bullying.

Zen emphasizes that worrying about the future is a complete waste of time. No one can predict the future. There never were any guarantees about the future. Why grieve for something that you never possessed?

"Do not pursue the past... Do not lose yourself in the future... The past no longer is... The future has not yet come... Looking deeply at life as it is..., " - the Buddha.

In today's economy, few jobs really are "secure." The average worker will work in many jobs during his or her career. Even Steve Jobs, the founder of Apple, Inc., the world-wide computer behemoth, was fired and he founded the place. I knew a tenured college professor who lost her job after 20 years when her college decided that it would no longer offer instruction in the language she taught. Prior to this, she never gave a thought to the possibility of being terminated. There are many reasons that jobs today are no longer secure.

Your company could be acquired by another company, rendering your job redundant. The chief financial officer could embezzle all of the company's funds and force the company into bankruptcy. The company could move to another state that offers a better tax incentive.

Some unscrupulous employers have no loyalty to anything but the bottom line.

After his enlightenment, the Buddha is pictured holding a lotus flower, a symbol of wisdom. A lotus bloom is a beautiful flower that comes from muddied water. The muddy water in your case may be a job with an unscrupulous employer that tolerates bullying for strategic reasons – say to downsize without paying unemployment compensation.

A job today represents an impermanent relationship. But that is not inevitably bad news for workers. You might prosper more by leaving your job than by staying in it. Working for a bully is a terrible dead end. Research shows that targets stop being innovative and working hard for the company. They spend a lot of time sick, defending themselves, and responding to the bully's allegations. It is quite possible that you could transition into a new phase of life that is more fulfilling and fruitful. You might find a job in a workplace where the employer values its employees and treats them with dignity and respect.

There is a story about an old farmer whose horse ran away. Upon hearing the news, his neighbors came to visit.

"Such bad luck," they said sympathetically.

"We'll see," said the farmer.

The horse returned the next morning, bringing with it three other wild horses.

"How wonderful," said the neighbors.

"We'll see," said the farmer.

The next day, the farmer's son tried to ride one of the wild horses. The boy was thrown to the ground and broke his leg.

The neighbors offered their sympathy for the farmer's misfortune.

"We'll see," said the farmer.

Military officers came to the village to draft young men into the army. They passed by the farmer's son after they noticed his leg was broken.

The neighbors congratulated the farmer on his good fortune.

"We'll see" said the farmer.

The point of the story is that one never knows whether an event or occurrence ultimately will be bad or good in the context of a lifetime. When one is enmeshed in a difficult workplace, it is useful to maintain a balanced perspective. This is one job among many that you will probably have over the years.

Chapter 5

THE PUPPET MASTER

"The fool thinks he has won a battle when he bullies with harsh speech, but knowing how to be forbearing alone makes one victorious."

- *the Buddha*

John's boss frequently blows up at him, belittles him and unfairly criticizes John's work.

On Monday, his boss told John to work on a project that John (not his real name) knew could not be accomplished by the assigned deadline. John attempted to raise this concern but his boss cut him off. "I know this will interfere with your video games or pornography or whatever else you do on the computer all day but I need this... Do it or pack your things and get out," said his boss.

Despite his best efforts, John could not pull together the information from diverse sources that was necessary to meet the deadline. Given his boss' threat, John was anxious and worried about his job.

At a department-wide meeting, John's boss told the unit director, with obvious disdain, that the entire project was delayed because one team member hadn't finished his work on time. He turned and looked at John, who was sitting beside him, and everyone else in the room followed suit.

Something in John snapped.

John stood up so quickly that his chair back flew back and hit the wall with a loud thwack. Pointing his trembling finger a few inches from his boss's face, John shouted, "That's bullshit. I told you there wasn't enough time."

John's boss raised his arms in a defensive posture, as if to fend off an imminent blow.

At that point, the departmental director stood up and shouted, "I'll have no more of this!" To John, he said, "Go to your office immediately and wait there."

A half hour later, the company's human resources officer handed John a written warning and a three-day suspension. He said John's actions were unprofessional and threatening. He asked John several questions about John's mental state, as if John were psychologically disturbed. He told John to get anger management counseling if he wished to continue working at the company.

Instead of being perceived as a target of bullying, John now was seen as a hotheaded employee with anger management problems. It was almost as if John's boss was a puppet master, pulling strings from behind a curtain in a children's melodrama.

Anger is not always a bad thing. It is an emotion that can alert you to a problem and it can propel you to act constructively to resolve a problem. In the context of workplace abuse, however, anger can be dangerous.

If you are not careful, anger about a bullying boss or employer can propel you to act against your own self-interest.

Targets of workplace abuse almost always regret sending a bullying boss a scathing email or leaving a scorched-earth incendiary voice-mail. These communications inevitably become evidence that is used by the bully against the target.

As the Buddha observed:

"Holding on to anger is like grasping a hot coal with the intent of throwing it at someone else; you are the one who gets burned."

It is far better to recognize that you are angry and to use this realization as a warning sign to wait until you calm down before making a response. With a cool head, John could have developed a constructive and reasonable response to the bullying, possibly shifting some or the entire fault to his boss for assigning work at the last minute with an unrealistic deadline.

A better course of action might have been to initially send his boss a respectful and carefully worded email stating:

"Regarding our meeting this morning, you informed me that this project is due on X date and I will make every effort to meet that deadline. However, as I attempted to tell you, I am concerned there is insufficient time to complete the project by the deadline for reasons that are outside of my control. These reasons include ... That said, I assure you that I will do everything possible to meet the deadline."

When he was criticized for failing to meet the deadline, John could have effectively made the case that his boss assigned him the work too late and so he was unable to meet the deadline for reasons beyond his control, and that his boss knew the deadline was unrealistic.

In Zen theory destructive emotions are considered obstacles that need to be eliminated through meditation and mindfulness in order to find happiness. According to Buddhist author Ani Thubten Chodron:

> "In the moment of anger's arising in our body-mind complex, at first there is just an energy, a feeling, the merest glimmer of an experience; it has not yet devolved into violence and aggression. We can learn to deal with it, through mindful awareness coupled with patience, self-observation and introspection."

No Puppets in Zen

The late British philosopher Alan Watts observed that religions promulgate the image of humanity as puppets who are created in the manner that a potter fashions a bowl out of clay. "Submission to fate implies someone who submits, someone who is the helpless puppet of circumstances," writes Watts, adding, "for Zen there is no such person."

Watts said people feel themselves to be puppets because they separate "themselves" from their minds, thinking that their nature is somehow involuntarily thrust upon "them."

Watts observed that the moon shines upon the water and, completely independently, the water reflects the moon. The water does not *intend* to receive the image of the moon, nor does the moon *intend* to cast its reflection on the water. And when there is no moon or water there is no moon-in-water. Like the moon and the water, Watts said, the nature of the mind and senses are independent of external experiences.

Watt's theory boils down to this. A target of workplace bullying does not have to react to abuse like a puppet on a string.

Targets can choose how they will react to workplace bullying. Nothing is preordained.

Whether and how an individual reacts to abuse is completely up to the individual. The "self" that we construct in our minds is essentially an *idea* that is formed through the culmination of past experience. An idea is not fixed.

John's impulsive reaction to his boss' goading was unnecessarily destructive because John acted against his own self interest. John could have avoided this by perceiving himself as a deliberative and rational human being who cannot be goaded into responding rashly in the heat of anger.

There is a Zen story about a university professor who visited an old Zen master to learn about Zen. The master poured the professor a cup of tea. When the cup was full, the master kept on pouring. The professor watched as the tea overflowed the cup and dripped onto the table and floor.

"It is overfull. No more will go in!" said the professor.

"Like this cup," the master said, "you are full of your own opinions and speculations. How can I show you Zen unless you first empty your cup?"

To gain the benefits of Zen, it is necessary to empty one's mind of preconceived notions and to be open-minded and willing to look at things in a different way.

Human Resources

John had sensed that he was being bullied for weeks but he was either in denial, reluctant or unable to confront the issue. Or maybe he thought it would just go away. Workplace abuse is like mold growing in the damp behind a wall. It doesn't just go away. Even if it is not visible, it keeps growing and spreading. Meanwhile, the target's ability to cope with abuse diminishes under the cumulative weight of anxiety and stress.

Under Zen theory, hostility is never a good response to hostility.

> *"Hostilities aren't stilled through hostility, regardless. Hostilities are stilled through non-hostility: this, an unending truth," said the Buddha.*

When John first began to suspect he was being bullied, he could have chosen to act constructively.

John could have started a notebook or journal in which he recorded each incident of abuse. Every entry would include a date and time and whether there were witnesses present. He also could have recorded his feelings about the incident and why he felt his boss acted inappropriately. At some point, a pattern of bullying would emerge from these diverse incidents. John could have gathered allies – co-workers – who witnessed his boss's ill treatment. He might have discovered that other co-workers felt badly treated by John's boss. Meanwhile, John could have researched the problem of bullying in the workplace to become more knowledgeable about the problem.

Addressing the broader pattern of workplace bullying and abuse is a more effective course of action than complaining about a specific incident. When a worker goes to the human resources director, the unemployment office or a court of law with an isolated complaint, it is easy for the official reviewing the complaint to discount the validity of the criticism or even to blame the target. That is because a single complaint often comes down to a question of credibility – and the boss will usually win on that score because s/he has the mantle of supervisory authority.

Unless there is clear and egregious abuse, many officials are loath to second-guess the boss, who has the benefit of supervisory authority.

The reluctance of an official to support a target becomes far less problematic when a worker presents clear evidence of a series of abusive incidents that constitute a pattern of bullying.

John chose to impulsively respond to his boss's goading and the inadequate project deadline and his response was clearly inappropriate. After his outburst, the timeliness of the deadline became irrelevant. John was the problem.

Workers in the United States must be careful and deliberate when they respond to bullying by a supervisor. As previously noted, U.S. workers do not have a right to be treated with dignity and respect in the workplace as do their counterparts in Europe. Most workers can be fired for any reason, as long as it does not specifically violate a law. (i.e. discrimination or wages/hour laws). Workplace bullying is not illegal unless it is tied specifically to discrimination against a member of a protected class (i.e., race, sex, age or disability). And even valid discrimination claims are routinely dismissed by federal judges, who, coincidentally, have lifetime tenure.

In many lawsuits, judges have ruled that egregious instances of bullying were too trivial for legal redress. For example, a salesperson for a Utah company that specialized in business coaching was "tortured" by his supervisor during a training exercise. Waterboarding is recognized internationally as a form of torture. Salesman Chad Hudgens was asked to lie down with his head pointed downhill, and he was restrained by co-workers as water was poured over his face. He told a newspaper, "I'm trying to squirm, get out of this, no one's letting go." Then, his boss allegedly said, "Now guys, you see how hard Chad was struggling for a breath of air, how hard he was trying to breathe? That's how hard I want you to go. Get back on the phones and make some sales!" The judge granted the company's motion and *dismissed* a lawsuit filed by Hudgens that alleged, among other things, that he suffered extreme emotional distress. The Utah Supreme Court reversed the dismissal on a technicality that had nothing to do with the lawsuit's merits and the matter was subsequently settled.

A target is well advised to keep careful records that document a pattern of abuse. John failed to do this. His one instant of impulsive anger caused the tables to turn in his workplace dynamic of workplace abuse. Suddenly, John was on the defensive, fighting for his job. In a sense, John's worst enemy was John and not his boss.

Type of Bullying

Under Zen theory, the target of bullying is encouraged to react with compassion and kindness to the bully. This does not mean that a target of bullying should accept abusive behavior. To do so could invite illness or lead to the target's ouster from the workplace. The Buddha recognized that people need to make a living. Still, it is wise to understand what motivates an abusive boss.

> "Hate never ceases by hatred. Only love dispels hatred. This is an ancient and timeless law. It is better to conquer yourself than to win a thousand battles." said the Buddha.

Managers also bring baggage into the workplace. The boss may suffer from self-doubt and insecurity that causes him to need to be "right" all the time. The boss may have little or no training in management or may be following a model of abusive management that the boss endured earlier in his/her career. The boss may filter all of his/her experience through an ego that hungers to satisfy an insatiable inner need for recognition.

Understanding the boss's motivation can help a target craft an effective response to abuse.

Zen theory also holds that an abusive boss is suffering and will continue to suffer because no one can find happiness by inflicting harm on others. Such a person is ignorant and fails to understand that everything in the world is inter-related and interdependent. Also, the Buddha said: "The kind of seed sown will produce that kind of fruit. Those who do good will reap good results. Those who do evil will reap evil results." In other words, people who subject others to arrogant and humiliating treatment suffer the same fate themselves. The Buddha believed that no one wins when there is competition and greed: "If we win, we incur resentment toward ourselves. If we lose, our self-esteem is hurt."

The Dalai Lama, a Buddhist monk who was nominated for a Nobel Peace Prize, says, "You must not hate those who do wrong or harmful things; but with compassion, you must do what you can to stop them — for they are harming themselves, as well as those who suffer from their actions."

Understanding the abuser also helps the target place the bullying in perspective. Targets of workplace abuse often are loath to confront their abusers - sometimes with good reason. It would do little good to tell a sociopath to stop being a sociopath and it might invite more harm upon the target. However, confronting a manager who is clueless about the harmful impacts of his management techniques could result in change, especially if the manager felt that change would improve his standing or the department's performance.

A 2012 study by a team of Israeli researchers found that most targets try to avoid contact with an abusive supervisor but that this tactic may backfire because it increases the target's stress. According to the study, direct communication with a bully boss results in more positive emotions for the target than avoidance.

Use direct communication. Tell the bully that he or she must not treat you like that.

Avoiding the abuser tends to further increase the employee's stress because it is associated with a sense of weakness and perpetuates a fear of the supervisor.

Sadly, most workers do little or nothing about workplace abuse. It is almost as if they feel that workplace abuse is a kind of fate or destiny. A national 2012 study by CareerBuilder found that 35 percent of workers reported they have felt bullied on the job and 16 percent reported they suffered health-related problems as a result of bullying. However, only 27 percent of targets said they reported the bullying to their Human Resources department. Of these workers, 43 percent said action was taken while 57 percent said nothing was done. Seventeen percent of workers decided to quit their jobs to escape the situation.

Different types of Abuse

There are many different types of workplace abuse. It is not always about an individual bully. How a target responds to abuse should depend upon the type of bullying involved. There are generally three types of bullies in the American workplace:

1) Abusive managers. These managers may be threatened in some way by the target or they may be seeking to build their status within the company by achieving results through the exploitation of subordinates. A small percentage of abusive managers are actual psychopaths or sociopaths, lacking in empathy and unlikely to change.

2) Mobbing co-workers. These are co-workers, often led by one worker who is seeking status, who band together to bully and expel an "outsider." The leader lacks the supervisory authority of a boss but wields the authority of the unruly "mob."

3) Bullying employers. This is a little studied but critical aspect of workplace bullying and abuse. Clearly some employers make a strategic decision to get rid of good employees for

pragmatic reasons by making working conditions intolerable through bullying. There are many court cases involving scurrilous employers who targeted employees after they suffered a workplace injury or complained about poor or dangerous working conditions or improper pay. Unethical employers may be seeking to avoid a legal obligation, such as paying worker's compensation or unemployment insurance.

Regardless of the type of bullying involved, targets can use Zen techniques to lower their stress level and to release negative impulses and emotions that would otherwise build up like steam in a pressure cooker. This, in turn, helps targets formulate a reasoned response to the problem.

Chapter 6

MEDITATION

Many people are afraid to empty their minds

Lest they may plunge

into the void.

They do not know that

their own Mind is the void.

- Zen Master Huang-Po, China's Tang Dynasty

Long before the time of the Buddha, people have engaged in some form of meditation. Cave paintings that are time dated 15,000 years ago show shamans lying on the ground in a deep meditative state asking the spirits for a successful hunt. Yet, it is only in the past few decades that meditation has become well known in the West.

Daisetz Teitaro Suzuki (1870-1966), who lectured about Zen at American universities, is credited with bringing Zen to the West. Susuki was Japanese and the author of books and essays on Far Eastern philosophy, including Buddhism and Zen. His work was influential with so called "Beat Generation" poets and authors like Jack Kerouac.

Zen must be "directly and personally experienced by each of us in his inner spirit. Just as two stainless mirrors reflect each other, the fact and our own spirits must stand facing each other with no intervening agents."-D.T. Suzuki.

In his 1958 book, "The Dharma Bums," Kerouac writes about discovering Buddhism: "i suddenly felt that i had lived in a previous lifetime innumerable ages ago and now because of the faults and sins in that lifetime i was being degraded to a more grievous domain of existence and my karma was to be born in america where nobody has any fun or believes in anything, especially freedom."

Kerouac describes dharma bums as "refusing to subscribe to the general demand that they consume production and [they] have to work for the privilege of consuming all that crap they didn't really want anyway such as refrigerators, tv sets, cars, at least new fancy cars, certain hair oils and deodorants and general junk you finally always see a week later in the garbage anyway, all of them imprisoned in a system of work, produce, consume, work, produce, consume..."

A decade later, the Beatles shone a spotlight on Buddhism. John Lennon, Paul McCartney and George Harrison traveled to India in 1968 to attend an advanced Transcendental Meditation (TM) training session at the ashram of Maharishi Mahesh Yogi. Harrison said the group's unprecedented fame and riches had left him feeling unfulfilled. "Like, we're The Beatles after all, aren't we? We have all the money you could ever dream of. We have all the fame you could ever wish for. But, it isn't love. It isn't health. It isn't peace inside, is it?" he said.

Today at least 10 million Americans say they practice some form of meditation. There are more than 200 meditation-based stress reduction programs at major medical centers around the country. While meditation is not a prescription for happiness, there is a growing body of scientific evidence that meditation contributes to emotional well-being or, as George Harrison might say, "peace inside."

Stress and Illness

The ability to relieve stress and anxiety is perhaps the most well known benefit of meditation. That's no small thing in the context of workplace abuse. Job stress can lead to serious mental and/or physical health problems. When you are abused at work, you experience the equivalent of job stress on steroids. The longer the stress continues, the more likely it is that you will experience mental and/or physical health damage.

The damage caused by stress is both short term (e.g., depression, anxiety, insomnia) and long term. The Center for Promotion of Health in the New England

Workplace reports that chronic job stress can cause musculoskeletal disorders and even cardiovascular and other chronic diseases. The Centers for Disease Control (CDC) estimates that up to 23 percent of heart disease-related deaths per year could be prevented if the levels of job strain in the most stressful occupations were reduced to average levels present in other occupations. The CDC recommends, among other things, ensuring a respectful working environment for all workers.

Research shows that one of the most stressful aspects of any job involves the quality of the employer management team and supervisory personnel.

Swedish researchers at the Stress Institute in Stockholm in 2008 studied more than 3,100 men over a 10-year period in typical work settings. The researchers reported in the Journal of Occupational and Environmental Medicine that employees who had managers who were incompetent, inconsiderate, secretive and uncommunicative were 60 percent more likely to suffer a heart attack or another life-threatening cardiac condition. Employees who worked with "good" leaders were 40 percent less likely to suffer heart problems.

Unfortunately, many employers are ignorant of the devastating impact that poor managers have on the workplace or, worse, some employers don't care. There are unscrupulous employers that actually encourage bullying or abuse to get rid of good employees to avoid a legal duty, such as paying unemployment or worker's compensation. What's a worker to do? Meditation is increasingly recognized as an effective tool to counter the potential health problems that result from job stress.

Zen Benefits

Using advanced technology, scientists have shown that meditating not only relieves stress but can actually lead to healthy changes in the brain.

Scientists at Harvard University studied 16 participants in an 8-week Mindfulness-Based Stress Reduction Program meditation program. The scientists took magnetic resonance (MR) imaging scans of the brain structure of the participants two weeks before and after they participated in the program. These scans were compared to a set of MR scans taken of a control group of non-mediators. The researchers reported the following in 2011:

- Meditators reported a reduction in stress that was correlated with decreased gray-matter density in the amygdale, which is the source of the fight-or-flight response to perceived threat and stress.

- Increased gray-matter density was observed in the meditators' left hippocampus, which is important for learning and memory, and in structures associated with awareness compassion and introspection.

None of the above changes were noted in the control group.

Other research shows that workplace meditation can lead to mental and physical health improvements:

- Dr. Barbara Frederickson, a professor of psychology at the University of North Carolina, studied workers who used a type of "loving kindness" meditation in the workplace. She said that in just six weeks workers improved their "vagal tone," which refers to a part of the brain that relates to positive emotions. She said these workers had improved ability to pay attention and showed improved emotional health and more positive social behaviors. Just as an individual can improve muscle tone with physical training, she said, an individual can improve their emotional outlook by practicing meditation.

- Dr. Charles Raison, MD, clinical director of the Emory University Mind-Body Program, has studied the impact of compassion meditation ("lojong") on practitioners. This type of meditation is designed to foster empathy with others. Dr. Raison said that stress triggers inflammation in the human body, which can lead to depression, cancer and heart disease. People who practice compassion meditation "have less stress inflammatory reactivity and other stress responses. It's tied to how much they practice... The more you meditate, the more you benefit."

- Richard J. Davidson, a professor of psychiatry and director of the neuroscience laboratory at the University of Wisconsin, says brain scans show that meditation leads to increased capacity for compassion, both emotionally and in practice. One study showed that even novice practitioners became more altruistic as a result of meditation. "Even two weeks of training for 30 minutes a day can result in robust changes in brain and behavior," said Davidson.

Generally research shows that meditation may help to lower blood pressure and cholesterol, improve focus and concentration, enhance creativity and deepen the practitioner's sense of spirituality and purpose. In short, meditation can be an important tool to maintain health and well-being.

Inner peace?

Zen theory suggests that anyone can find "inner peace" regardless of external circumstances. What does this really mean? Should you expect that you will never again experience anxiety or fear if you meditate regularly? No.

Even enlightened people are not spared from life's adversity.

The Dalai Lama is almost always pictured smiling but his path in life has been difficult. He was forced to flee Tibet in 1959 after the country was occupied by the People's Republic of China. The Dali Lama established a community in exile in India that espouses a policy of nonviolence. He toiled for decades without success to engage China in negotiations in an effort to alleviate the suffering of Tibetans. Yet, the Dali Lama radiates peace, warmth and happiness.

The Dali Lama says that inner peace allows people to "face difficulties with calm and reason, while keeping our inner happiness." He writes that the antidote to hatred is tolerance, which allows one to refrain from acting angrily to harm inflicted upon you by others. "You could call this practice 'inner disarmament,' in that a well-developed tolerance makes you free from the compulsion to counterattack," he said.

Even the Buddha suffered after his enlightenment. According to one story, the Buddha had a cousin, Devadatta, who is said to have entered the Buddha's community of monks. Devadatta became increasingly conceited and intent on worldly gain and fame. One day, Devadatta asked the Buddha to make him the leader of the monks but the Buddha refused, causing Devadatta to feel anger and resentment toward him. Devadatta climbed a high mountain peak and threw a huge stone at the Buddha in an attempt to kill him. The stone hit another stone and splintered. Although the

Buddha escaped death, a shard of the rock pierced his foot, causing him excruciating pain. As the story goes, the Buddha lay down on his robe, on his right side, with one foot placed on top of the other. He was mindful, alert and impervious to the pain.

> *"The mind is everything. What you think you become," said the Buddha.*

Even if circumstances seem dire and hopeless, there may be a way to find hope. There is a Buddhist story about an aged man who went to the Buddha for advice. "I am old and decrepit... I am sick and constantly ailing. My body hurts all the time. What can I do to find happiness?" The Buddha told him to think in the following manner: 'Though I am ill in body, my mind shall not be ill.'" The aged man felt hopeful for the first time.

There is no doubt that being a target of workplace abuse is painful. It is not reasonable to expect that Zen will miraculously transform an excruciating employment environment into a pleasant and congenial workplace. But meditation can help a target restore a sense of calm and tranquility and diminish fear and irrationality. It might help you change the way you think and instill a sense of hope.

Are We There Yet?

Some people try Zen once or twice and conclude that it was not successful because they didn't emerge from meditation feeling as if they'd spent two weeks in the south of France. It is wise to anticipate that your fledgling efforts to meditate are the beginning of a journey and not the end. There is a Zen story about the sometimes arduous path to inner peace:

A goldsmith told his apprentice to remove the impurities from a gold sample. The apprentice poured the gold into a troth and cleaned it but there was still gravel, rocks and other impurities in the gold. The apprentice again washed and rinsed the gold. The gold was cleaner this time but there were still fine grains of sand and dust in the gold. Again, the apprentice washed and cleaned the gold. Finally, the gold seemed pure.

The goldsmith poured the gold into a melting pot, fanned it and smelted it. But the gold was not yet malleable. As the goldsmith continued to fan, melt and smelt the gold, the dross was finally removed. The gold became malleable, luminous and fit for work.

This story is a metaphor for the search for enlightenment. The apprentice did not find enlightenment merely by sitting under a Bodhi Tree. He needed to "refine" his mind by ridding it of "impurities" such as craving and desire.

A milestone in any meditation practice occurs with the realization that your thoughts are not "you." As your awareness increases, it becomes clear that people are not their emotions or fears. Our feelings are the outcome of an internal filtering process. It is roughly akin to the way people see a pattern in a Rorschach ink blot test. Individuals often come up with differing interpretations of an ink blot depending upon their personality and different psychological factors. One person will see a wolf in the ink blot while another will see a dancing bear. Your observations are filtered through the totality of your instincts and your experience.

Instead of reacting impulsively and perhaps incorrectly, Zen helps individuals free themselves from mistaken or delusionary thinking, prejudices and past and future fears by seeing things more clearly and calmly.

Here is a lovely poem that describes the illusive nature of the mind by Minemoto no Sanetomo, a Japanese shogun and poet who lived from 1203 – 1219:

Creations of the Mind...

The cold spring wind is fragrant with the scent

of the first flowering plum, and, as it blows,

the fragrance lingers in my garment's fold.

Some speak of Buddhas, some of countless gods;

What are they, but creations of the mind?

Put not your trust in anything you see:

All that you see, hear, feel, is but a dream.

121

Better a man confess his inmost sin,

than build a holy Temple to the gods.

The world's a dream, a cherry flower that blows,

and sheds its petal-snow, and is no more.

Spring verges on to summer; and the bloom,

that pleased my eye in April, is no more.

At midnight, in the glistening drops of dew

that sparkle on the lotus-petal, see

the moon's bright face reflected wholly there.

Possibility of More Stress

Meditation offers the promise of stress relief but there is a possibility that a worker will, at least initially, experience *more* stress.

Some workers come to meditation because they have a general feeling of angst about the workplace. In meditation, they recognize they feel anxious, angry and fearful. Possibly they have been in denial for months about what is happening to them. They may be aghast to realize they are not the target of a few isolated incidents of incivility but of intentional bullying. They may fear for the first time that the problem could lead to job loss.

Other workers come to the painful realization through meditation that they have played a significant role in the breakdown of the relationship with their co-workers, supervisor or employer. Perhaps they even realize that they have treated others abusively.

The Buddha taught that it is always better to address the truth head on. In fact, it is part of the Buddhist tradition for beginning meditators to spend significant time meditating on the bodies of corpses in cremation grounds to help them accept the inevitability and truth of death. Zen is the quest for truth, which is achieved by setting aside ignorance and avoidance.

Additional stress as a result of meditation may add to your anxiety level but remember that you are engaged in a journey and that the truth will allow you to respond to workplace abuse more effectively and may even help you salvage a job that would otherwise be lost to you.

Chapter 7

ZEN AT WORK

"Your worst enemy can not harm you as much as your own thoughts, unguarded. But once mastered, no one can help you as much, not even your father or your mother."

- the Buddha.

Meditation does not require a fancy chair or expensive pillow, mood lighting, the soothing sound of babbling water from a desktop fountain or a cone of silence. It can be done anywhere and anytime. It can be easily accomplished any time in an office, at a desk, in the elevator or during a ten-minute break. Anyone can benefit from engaging in meditation but it could be a lifesaver if you are stuck in a difficult workplace.

Yet, meditation is not like Hostetter's Celebrated Stomach Bitters, a miracle tonic that purported to cure every conceivable ailment in the 1800s. Meditation can help eliminate stress and provide more clarity in your life but you must put in the time and effort if you wish to see results.

It is helpful to begin meditation with realistic expectations. It could take time and practice to evict the negative emotion, judgments and thoughts that clutter your mind. This effort is rarely as easy as letting go of the string of a helium balloon. There are no shortcuts and you can't get ahead by working harder or more efficiently.

An old Buddhist story illustrates the challenge of beginning a meditation practice:

A young martial arts student went to his teacher and said he wanted to learn everything he could about the teacher's martial arts system. "How long will it take me to master it," the student asked.

The Master replied: "Ten years."

The student hesitated, obviously unsettled by the answer. "But Master, I plan to work very hard. I will practice ten hours or more a day. If I do all of this, how long will it take?"

"Twenty years," replied the Master.

The person who works the hardest is not guaranteed to achieve the benefits of medication the soonest; what is required is the right kind of effort. The meditator must submit to the idea of quieting the mind.

Meditation is even more of a challenge when you feel like you are under attack at work. However, it is important to remember that when the need is greatest so too are the rewards. Through meditation, you can learn to exercise a measure of control over a situation that typically is out of your hands.

Focus

Meditation essentially involves cultivating a focus on the present by eliminating the distractions that normally occupy our minds, including thoughts of greed, jealousy and hatred. In a sense, you are asking your mind to cooperate by focusing instead of doing what it wants to do.

According to Zen theory, the way people feel is not dictated by their "mind" but by what they choose to pay attention to and how they choose to respond. What is the mind? Some Buddhists define the mind as the place where thinking occurs.

Lama Zopa Rinpoche, a Tibetan Buddhist master, describes the mind as "a phenomenon that is not body, not substantial, has no form, no shape, no colour, but, like a mirror, can clearly reflect objects."

It might be easier to think about what the mind is not – it is not the various thoughts, opinions and emotions that pass through it at any moment.

Ordinarily, our minds are in a continuous whirl of activity as our thoughts jump from one topic, external stimuli and emotion to another. Our thoughts race through our minds like a tornado over a Midwest cornfield, collecting cows, assorted trucks and wood frame houses as it goes. Meanwhile, we make constant judgments. We deem something to be good, bad, sweet, malicious, hurtful, comforting, silly, deep, difficult, easy, etc. Many of us fret about the past and worry about the future, living in a kind of suspended animation, oblivious to the present.

When you are being mistreated at work, everything speeds up.

Targets of workplace abuse often inhabit a state of emotional hyper-drive.

Many targets report they think obsessively about the unfairness of their situation, their outrage, and their fears. Why me? How dare they? What if I'm fired? If you do nothing, anything can and will enter your mind. In a sense, you are vulnerable to "vagrant" thoughts and emotions. Your mind can be hijacked at any time by a random care or an irrational prejudice.

Mindlessness - the opposite of mindfulness – is sometimes defined as the rigid adherence to old patterns of thought. So when X happens, your mind retrieves a response that was perhaps appropriate five years ago when Y happened. Never mind that X and Y are occurring at a different time under completely different circumstances.

Meditation helps people to live more intentionally by being less subject to the pull of random, scattered and confused feelings and thoughts. For example, Inez's boss extolled her virtues at her annual performance review. Then he suggested that she could improve in one area. Inez left the meeting feeling devastated. If it had been a test in school, she would have scored 95 out of 100. So what's the problem?

Inez (not her real name) grew up in poverty. It took her six years to put herself through college, working full time. She is a single mother with two small children who depend on her. Her salary finances a mortgage and car payment. When Inez heard her boss' criticism, she felt her accomplishments, possessions and even her future were in danger of slipping away. Instead of hearing what her boss actually said, she heard what she feared the most.

Meditation offers practitioners the possibility of clarity and perspective. This enables the practitioner to respond to a circumstance in a way that leads to well-being rather than anguish and difficulty. This awareness fosters a sense of rationality, calm and even tranquility. Suppose your boss said or did something that you perceived as aggressive and unfair. Before responding impulsively to this perceived slight, you might ask yourself:

- What does this really mean?

- Is this out of character for my boss?

- Is he or she having a bad day?

- Could my boss have misunderstood something that I did?

- Was I out of line?

- Did I misunderstand my boss?

– What type of response, if any, is warranted?

According to John Teasdale, an English scientist who studied mindfulness-based cognitive therapy, mindfulness is a habit. "It's something the more one does, the more likely one is to be in that mode with less and less effort... it's a skill that can be learned ... What's difficult is to remember to be mindful," said Teasdale.

Hindrances

Freeing the mind of distractions is like emptying a space. In meditation, one learns to observe distractions when they arise without reacting to them or making judgments about them, thus depriving distractions of the ability to take over one's thoughts.

Imagine a museum wall filled with dozens of disconnected paintings of all genres, skill levels and time periods. The result is overwhelming – a cacophony of images. As you remove the paintings, you begin to notice the hue of the white paint on the wall, the shadows created by spot lighting, the size and shape of the room, etc. When all the paintings are gone except one, you are stunned. It is a masterpiece painted in 1900 by the Impressionist painter Claude Monet in Giverny, France. It is a colorful summer garden scene. You notice Monet's color palette, the thickness of the paint on the canvas and the effervescence of this beautiful natural setting. The painting was there all along but you never saw it in the confusion of artwork on the wall.

In Buddhist doctrine, there are five traditional hindrances or obstacles to meditation. These hindrances are what stand between you and your awareness of the Monet masterpiece on the wall.

The Five Hindrances to Meditation are:

1. "Sense desire" or craving,

2. Anger,

3. "Sloth and torpor" or sluggishness,

4. "Agitation and worry," and

5. "Extreme skepticism" or self-doubt about your ability to meditate.

Generally, Buddhists believe that the major impediment to achieving enlightenment is ego or "clinging" to the concept of self. Ego leads to selfishness, which, in Buddhist theory, prevents enlightenment and continues the cycle of human suffering through reincarnation. In Buddhist theory, there is no "self" - we are all part of "one mind."

In *Eight Verses for Training the Mind*, poet Kadampa Geshe Langri Tangpa (1054–1123) provides insight into the Buddhist perspective. Here are some of the verses:

> Whenever I interact with someone,
> May I view myself as the lowest amongst all,
> And, from the very depths of my heart,
> Respectfully hold others as superior.

> In all my deeds may I probe into my mind,
> And as soon as mental and emotional afflictions arise-
> As they endanger myself and others-
> May I strongly confront them and avert them.

When others, out of jealousy
Treat me wrongly with abuse, slander, and scorn,
May I take upon myself the defeat
And offer to others the victory.

When someone whom I have helped,
Or in whom I have placed great hopes,
Mistreats me in extremely hurtful ways,
May I regard him still as my precious teacher.

Unlike serious Buddhists, you may not be especially concerned about the possibility of reincarnation as a cockroach or wild boar. However, it is a fundamental tenet of most, if not all, of the world's religions that people have a responsibility to help one another and to live in such a way as to make the world a better place. Freeing the mind provides space for compassion, even compassion for a bully.

The Ego

Ego is a noteworthy source of anguish in the workplace. Bad bosses often share a common delusion that they are more competent and important than

135

anyone else, which is how they justify treating others in a demeaning and dismissive fashion. Employees may have an unrealistic idea about their own skill level and an exalted sense of their worth, causing them to fret that they are not paid enough or accorded more deference than co-workers.

Some Buddhists say the most valuable insight offered by meditation involves the phenomenon of cause and effect. This is the idea that what put out into the world will come back to you. You may come to recognize through meditation that many of your thoughts involve fear. People who are afraid tend to see the world as a scary and dangerous place. This insight may help you adjust your attitude so that you don't automatically respond in fear when there is no reason to be afraid. What if you are lonely because you have difficulty getting along with others? Through meditation, you may realize that you tend to view co-workers as a stepping stone to advancement, rather than a potential source of companionship and friendship.

This realization may help you adjust your attitude to become more genuine and likeable to others.

If you embrace the world with kindness and compassion, you may be surprised see kindness and compassion at work in the world.

The Dalai Lama suggests that anyone can be happier in their job if they move toward a deeper understanding of the job. He teaches that the highest purpose of work, and indeed life, is helping others. The Dalai Lama advises workers to go beyond their job title, duties and the perks of the job and think about how they can make a meaningful contribution to others or society.

Types of Meditation

The Buddha did not discover meditation. Some historians say ancient hunting and gathering societies discovered meditation and its different states of consciousness while gazing into the flames of their fires. The earliest written records of the practice of meditation are said to be from China at around 5000

BC. Meditation appears in some guise in cultures all over the world. Arguably, meditation is part of many religious traditions, including Buddhism, Taoism, Christianity and Judaism.

There are many different types of meditation.

A traditional Zen meditation is called, "zazen," which means seated meditation. This a "mindfulness" or "open monitoring" meditation in which practitioners typically sit quietly and observe, non-judgmentally, thoughts, feelings, or whatever arises moment to moment.

Meditators use different "tools" to help them focus. These include:

- Counting breath sounds.
- Focusing on a picture or statue of a holy figure, such as the Buddha, Jesus Christ, or a saint.
- Picturing a healing energy or a peaceful place.
- Reading a reflective or inspirational writing.
- Contemplating nature.

Alternatively, some meditators practice a type of "controlled focus" meditation. This involves concentrating on a concept such as loving-kindness and compassion for others. Researchers have studied veteran Buddhist monks and found that concentrating on "loving kindness and compassion" increased those feelings as well as focus.

Another form of meditation, "Transcendental Meditation" (TM), became popular in the 1960s when rock stars flocked to India to study with Maharishi Mahesh Yogi. TM is a type of "automatic self-transcending" meditation that is based on the ancient Buddhist Vedic tradition. It involves repeating a mantra – a word that is meaningful chiefly because of its sound – over and over again. Practitioners are encouraged to meditate for 20 minutes twice a day while sitting comfortably with eyes closed. There is no attempt to direct or control one's thoughts. The objective of the meditative exercise is to achieve a spontaneous transcendent state in which there is no intentional mental activity. TM is said to be effective in alleviating chronic stress and anxiety. Research also shows that TM can lower blood pressure that leads to hypertension. TM centers and trained instructors are located in almost every community.

The following chapters contain a selection of meditations that are intended to help workers who are suffering from workplace bullying and abuse or who find themselves stuck in a difficult and dispiriting workplace.

These meditations could help you put your situation in a more positive light, and perhaps even help you move toward a favorable resolution to your workplace problems.

Chapter 8

FIRST STEPS

Meditate.
Live purely. Be quiet.
Do your work with mastery.
Like the moon, come out
from behind the clouds!
Shine
　　　- the Buddha

According to Buddhist doctrine, there are eight steps to mindfulness – beginner's mind, non-judgment, acknowledgement, non-striving, equanimity, letting be, self-reliance and self-compassion. Perhaps the most important of these is the first – beginner's mind.

It is important to accept that you are a novice and to approach the task with patience and persistence. If you are prepared to put forth effort and work through any problems you will succeed.

The challenge can be seen in an old Buddhist story about a man who captured six animals - a snake, crocodile, bird, dog, jackal and monkey. Each animal has a different habitat and feeding ground. The man tied them all to a strong rope and affixed the rope to a pillar. After a moment, each of the animals pulled in different directions toward their respective feeding grounds and habitats. The bird tried to fly into the sky. The dog strained to go to the village. The monkey wanted to enter the forest. The crocodiles searched for the sea. And the jackal tried to find the grassy open plains. The animals eventually became fatigued and lay down.

Your senses are like the animals, pulling in different directions. When a sound arises, your mind goes to the sound. Or it travels to the pain in your lower back, the scent of an orange or the memory of something beautiful.

Your senses normally vie for your mind's attention and this can make meditation a challenge.

Unlike the man with six animals, you can't tie your senses to a pillar. You can, however, eliminate distractions that impede meditation and calm your senses. Eventually all of the "animals" lie down peacefully as you become immersed in a meditative state.

Here are some general preliminary steps to prepare for meditation:

1) Remind yourself that it is important during meditation to refrain from making judgments or engaging in grasping and striving behaviors. In other words, prepare to observe things as they are, and then let them be.

2) Align your head, neck, and back in a straight line as best you can, while remaining comfortable. Try not to rest your back on the chair. Place your hands in whatever position is comfortable. Some people emulate the Buddha

by placing their left hand in their lap, palm up, under their right hand, palm up, with the thumbs lightly touching each other. Others place their hands on their thighs.

3) Place your feet flat on the floor.

4) Close your eyes or cast your eyes downward. If you are concerned about time, place a clock or your watch nearby you so that you can refer to it.

5) Some meditators place their tongue at the top of their mouth or behind their front teeth. Some meditators form their lips into a half-smile to emulate the Buddha.

6) Gather up your attention as you would pull a jacket tightly when chilled. Recognize that the mind has a tendency to wander. It is natural to think about a doctor's appointment or a work assignment during meditation. If your mind strays, gently return your awareness to the present.

7) Be comfortable. If you feel physical pain, it is okay to shift your position. Alternatively, you can incorporate the pain into your meditation and observe these painful sensations non-judgmentally.

8) If you feel drowsy, open your eyes more fully or change your posture. For example, you might find it better to stand up. Possibly you need to sleep. If so, meditate later when you are feeling rested.

After reviewing the simple instructions for Mindfulness Meditation in the next chapter, you will be ready to begin. You may also find it useful to try the guided meditations on self-compassion and compassion for your enemy. If you like, read these guided meditations and pause where appropriate to repeat the short italicized verses.

You also will find references to other types of meditative techniques, such as a walking meditation or an image or sound-based meditation. Plus, there are meditative prayers to provide fodder for thought.

Feel free to revise any meditation to suit your special needs.

Chapter 9

MINDFULNESS MEDITATION

"Nothing can harm you as much as your own thoughts unguarded." – *the Buddha*

Zen theory holds that we live in a state akin to "darkness" most of the time because we are preoccupied with the past and the future. Many Americans are caught up in the empty promise of materialism, hoping that the more possessions they own, the better they will feel. As you meditate, your mind lights up. Your focus increasingly narrows until you are in the present moment. Annoyances, disturbances and distractions fade away like shadows and you experience increasing clarity and peace. This is "mindfulness" or intense awareness of each consecutive moment, including our bodily feelings, emotions, thoughts and observations.

This chapter includes a guided mindfulness meditation that will help you achieve a state of peace and relaxation.

The goal of "mindfulness meditation" is not only to become aware of the present but to accept it without judging. You may *feel* bad, for example, but that does not mean that you *are* bad. Through meditation, you become aware of how you feel without attributing a meaning to your feeling.

Mindfulness meditation is a simple and easy form of meditation. It is particularly good for people who work in a difficult environment because it can easily be done in an office, seated behind a desk. In fact, one can practice mindfulness at any time - while brushing your teeth, as your car idles at a stop light or during the elevator ride to the top floor.

"Be mindful!" the Buddha exhorted his followers.

All you need for this meditation are your lungs, air to breathe and some patience.

Here and Now

Mindfulness means to be aware of what is actually happening at the successive moments of perception. Mindfulness strips away the unessential. It involves being in the here and now.

Jon Kabat-Zinn, founder of an eight-week Mindfulness-Based Stress Reduction program at the University of Massachusetts Medical Center, puts it this way:

> Mindfulness means paying attention in a
> particular way;
> on purpose,
> in the present moment, and
> nonjudgmentally.

Kabat-Zinn was a pioneer of the concept of using mindfulness-based meditation specifically to reduce stress in the late 1970s, along with Saki Santorelli, Ph.D. and other colleagues at the University of Massachusetts Medical Center. There are now mindfulness-based stress reduction programs in major hospitals across the country.

Mindfulness is the "unfailing master key" for knowing the mind.

Mindfulness meditation requires cultivating the ability to observe the world without judgment. According to Buddhist master Luang Por Sumeho, non-judgmental observation means the following:

> "You only need the confidence to reflect, to be aware, not of how things *should be* but on what you are actually experiencing, without claiming it, without adding to it in any way. Thus, when I feel sad if I think 'I am sad' then I have made it more than what it is. Instead, I am simply aware of the sadness... So awareness exists without arising of thought."

In the Buddhist tradition, mindfulness is a tool to gain deep insight into oneself and the human condition. According to the Buddhist scholar and monk Nayanaponika Thera, mindfulness is "the unfailing master key for knowing the mind, and is thus the starting point; the perfect tool for shaping the mind, and is thus the focal point; the lofty manifestation of the achieved freedom of the mind, and is thus the culminating point."

It should be noted that while mindfulness meditation is rooted in Buddhism, it is not exclusive to that tradition. Aspects of mindfulness, including its emphasis on being in the present moment, are incorporated in some ways in many different religions, including Christianity and Judaism.

Mindfulness is not a mystical state. It is a form of concentrated attention that anyone can achieve. Mindfulness occurs after the mind is cleansed of distractions or impurities. Distractions include emotions, intellectual prejudices, assumptions and wishful thinking. Mindfulness helps practitioners to live in the present and be less reactive and more contemplative.

With mindfulness comes the ability to see the world as it unfolds moment by moment. You may feel unexpected joy in discovering the splendor of a ray of sunshine. You may discover something about yourself that went unnoticed in the frantic pace of everyday life. Perhaps a strength. Perhaps a shortcoming. You may gain insight into why you are experiencing workplace difficulties and how to better handle this problem.

In an ideal world, you would set aside 20 minutes or more once or twice a day to meditate. In a busy workplace, however, you might be lucky to find ten minutes. That's okay. Even five minutes is beneficial. Don't be anxious if you can't find a significant block of time to meditate each day. You will find it worthwhile if you meditate for even a few minutes here and there. The more you practice meditation, the more effective it will be - even if it is only for a short time each day.

I. GUIDED MINDFULNESS MEDICATION

The focus of Mindfulness Meditation is your breath. Take a moment to consider how fortunate you are to be able to breathe freely. The ability to breathe is fundamental to our physical and mental well-being. Many people suffer from health conditions that impede their ability to breathe. Be thankful for this blessing; it is ultimately much more important than any transitory struggle.

1) Sit upright, with your feet flat on the floor and your eyes cast downward. (*See* Chapter 8, Preliminary Steps)

2) Take a deep breath through your nose and release the breath through your mouth. Be aware of the breath entering and leaving your body. Let your attention be carried by your breath. Feel the sensation of each consecutive breath.

3) Notice if your body feels tense. Locate the points of tension in your body and picture these

areas as becoming more relaxed. Feel your jaw line soften. Allow your hands to rest effortlessly on your lap or thighs. Relax your body.

Remember - There is nothing better that you can do at this moment.

4) Keep your awareness on the natural flow of your breath as it travels in and out of your body. Is your breath firm and steady? Is your breath shallow and quick? Notice how you are breathing but don't allow your conscious mind to alter the rate or force of your breath. Just let it be what it is. Your breath will slow down naturally as you relax.

5) As you breathe slowly and gently, notice the momentary gap between each inhale and exhale. Allow each breath to bring you closer to peace and clarity.

6) If your mind wanders, observe whatever thoughts or emotions arise without judgment. These random thoughts have no substance. They are like an image in a mirror, an echo in a

154

canyon or a shimmering mirage in a desert. Simply pay witness to your breath.

7) Don't be dismayed if you have persistent thoughts or emotions or if you feel bored or even agitated. This is neither a problem nor a failing. It's just how you feel at that moment. This may be a sign that you have unresolved and important issues that you need to pay attention to. Gently return your attention to your breath.

8) If you can't shake a feeling of dread and fear, that's okay. It is better to acknowledge your feelings than to avoid them or run away from them. They are not real. They are like the reflection of the moon in the water. Try to let them go and return your awareness to your breath.

9) If you hear a sound that interrupts your focus – a car horn or a peal of laughter - gently return your awareness back to your breath. (In a particularly noisy office setting, you might

consider using sound-cancelling ear buds or headphones.)

10) Continue to breathe, slowly and softly. You are in the present, here and now. There is nothing else to do or to change. Each instant unfolds in its own time. Your mind is in a natural state of being.

11) Every breath flows outward like the concentric circles that occur when a dragonfly touches the still surface of a pond. Each breath sends energy out into the universe of which we are all a part. Your breath is seamless. Effortless.

12) As you breathe in and out, observe the way you feel in this calm place. Take this feeling with you into your day.

13) Open your eyes. Your meditation comes to an end. Has your anxiety lessened? Do you feel a sense of peace and joy? Thank yourself for taking this precious time to restore your spirits. Meditation represents an act of love and kindness toward yourself.

14) Repeat the following: May all the world and every living being in it feel at peace.

Go back to work determined to retain the sense of clarity and inner peace that you cultivated in this brief meditative exercise. Remember that you control how you respond to external pressures and instigations. You can choose to respond to provocations with intentional and calm deliberateness rather than with rash and potentially self-destructive impulsiveness.

II. SHARPENING YOUR FOCUS

In the beginning, meditation can be challenging. You are asking yourself to remain consciously aware of what is occurring in each successive moment. To be aware of your breath, your body engaged in the process of breathing, the feeling of sitting in a chair, your state of being juxtaposed with the outside world and, of course, the outside world. All the while, you are attempting to maintain an objective detachment and refrain from reacting and judging.

The mind is a powerful engine that usually pulls the train, not follows in back.

You are attempting to build awareness by imposing on your mind an intense focus on the present. Meditation is not always easy in the best of circumstances but you are sitting in a workplace where you may feel unsettled and unsafe.

There are tools to help you sharpen your focus.

Some people find it helpful to count their breath from one to ten and then repeat the count as time allows. You can count your breathe as you inhale and exhale. For example:

Inhale, one. Exhale, one.

Inhale, two. Exhale, two.

Or you can count your breath only when you exhale, like this:

Inhale –

Exhale – One

Inhale –

Exhale – Two.

In either case, when you reach ten, start the count over again from the beginning. Repeat the cycle as time permits.

Some people find it calming to center their awareness upon their stomach, breathing from the belly rather than the chest. This is called "diaphragmatic breathing" and is marked by expansion of the abdomen rather than the chest when breathing.

Under stress, people tend to take quick and shallow breaths. People who suffer panic attacks, for example, may experience shortness of breath. When you breathe from your stomach, you tend to breathe more deeply. This can have a calming effect. Center your awareness on your stomach as it expands and contracts.

Alternatively, you can focus upon your "heart center" or your chest. Feel your chest expand with air as you inhale, and then slowly contract as you exhale.

If you struggle and feel discouraged, consider undertaking a more traditional meditation practice in the comfort of your home or in another space, such as a Zen meditation center or studio. You may wish to pick a specific time each day to meditate and spend at least 20 minutes in meditation.

Sit in a chair or on a firm cushion. Some people prefer to kneel or even lie down.

Some meditators sit with one foot on their opposite thigh in what is known as a "half-lotus" position or they place both feet on opposite thighs in what is known as the "full lotus" position. The lotus position emulates the posture used by the Buddha in his search for enlightenment.

III. Reflections by the Buddha

The Twin Verses

The mind is the basis for everything.

Everything is created by my mind, and is ruled by my mind.

When I speak or act with impure thoughts, suffering follows me.

As the wheel of the cart follows the hoof of the ox.

The mind is the basis for everything.

Everything is created by my mind, and is ruled by my mind.

When I speak or act with a clear awareness, happiness stays with me.

Like my own shadow, it is unshakeable.

———

The Mind

My mind is trembling and unsteady,
Difficult to guard and difficult to restrain.
I straighten my thoughts
Like a fletcher* straightening arrows.

162

Just like a fish thrashes about
When taken from its home in the water and thrown on
dry land,
So my mind trembles and twists,
When taken from the world of illusion into meditation.

My mind is difficult to control.
Flighty and wild, it lands wherever it likes.
It is wonderful to control my mind,
Because a well-tamed mind brings happiness.

My mind is difficult to detect.
Very subtle, it slips away to wherever it likes.
When I am wise, I guard my mind,
Because a guarded mind brings happiness.

My thoughts wander far and wide, traveling alone,
Bodiless and naked, sheltering in a cave within me.
When I master my thoughts,
I will be freed from the bonds of illusion.

When my thoughts are unsteady,
When I forget the Way of Enlightenment,
When my dedication wavers,
Then my wisdom cannot grow.

When my thoughts are free from passions,
Free from covetous thoughts and ill-will,
When I abandon judgments of right and wrong,
Then, ever-watchful, I will have no fear.

* A fletcher is someone who makes archery products.

**Source: The Dhammapada: A Practitioner's Translation, Wikisource "The Free Library" Religious Texts, available at http://www.freemedialibrary.com/index.php/The_Dhamm apada:_A_Practitioner%27s_Translation

———

The Mind

It is good to tame the mind, which is difficult to hold in and flighty, rushing wherever it listeth;

a tamed mind brings happiness.

Let the wise man guard his thoughts, for they are difficult to perceive, very artful, and they rush wherever they list:

thoughts well guarded bring happiness.

Those who bridle their mind which travels far, moves about alone, is without a body, and hides in the chamber (of the heart),

will be free from the bonds of Mara (the tempter).

If a man's thoughts are unsteady, if he does not know the true law,

if his peace of mind is troubled, his knowledge will never be perfect.

If a man's thoughts are not dissipated, if his mind is not perplexed, if he has ceased to think of good or evil,

then there is no fear for him while he is watchful.

Knowing that this body is (fragile) like a jar, and making this thought firm like a fortress,

one should attack Mara (the tempter) with

the weapon of knowledge, one should watch him when conquered, and should

never rest.

* *The Project Gutenberg EBook of The Dhammapada, by Unknown.* Translator: F. Max Muller, available at http://www.gutenberg.org/files/2017/2017-h/2017-h.htm.

Wakefulness

Wakefulness is the way to life.

The fool sleeps

As if he were already dead,

But the Master is awake.

And he lives forever.

He watches.

He is clear.

How happy he is!

For he sees that wakefulness is life.

How happy he is,

Following the path of the awakened.

With Great perseverance

He meditates, seeking

Freedom and happiness.

Teachings of the Buddha, Shambhala Publications (2004), quoting Gautama Buddha, from the Dhhammapada, translated by Thomas Byrom.

Chapter 10

SELF COMPASSION MEDITATION

"You can search throughout the entire universe for someone who is more deserving of your love and affection than you are yourself, and that person is not to be found anywhere. You, yourself, as much as anybody in the entire universe, deserve your love and affection."

- the Buddha

If you had a good friend who was being bullied or abused in the workplace, would you notice her suffering? How would you counsel that friend? Would you be harsh and critical and point out your friend's inadequacies and failures? Would you tell her to "man up" or just get over it? Or would you be kind and caring and try to ease her suffering? In all likelihood, you would sympathize with your friend's suffering and let her know that you are there to support her through this difficult time.

Too often, targets of workplace bullying criticize and blame themselves. They fail to be as kind and compassionate to themselves as they would be to others in similar circumstances. This self-blame and criticism adds to the stress they already feel, causes more harm, making it harder to respond effectively to workplace abuse.

The Dalai Lama said that we must first be kind to ourselves.

> *"[C]ompassion is the state of wishing that the object of our compassion be free of suffering... Yourself first, and then in a more advanced way the aspiration will embrace other,"* the Dalai Lama.

To have self-compassion, you first must recognize that you are suffering. We are all sensitive human beings who suffer when we are targets of abuse. Targets of workplace abuse who fail to recognize they are suffering can be beaten down until they incur potentially severe mental and physical damage.

It makes a tremendous difference when targets of abuse simply refrain from adding to their suffering by being kind to themselves.

Mistakes - I've made a few...

It's likely that you've made mistakes. Everyone does. But other employees make mistakes and presumably they are not being savaged in a hostile workplace environment. The fact that you are being abused does not mean that you deserve to be abused.

It also is possible that you are not the most attractive, intelligent, enthusiastic and creative employee at your workplace. But workers who are even farther from perfection than you are not being bullied. You do not deserve to be bullied because you make mistakes and are not perfect.

In reality, you could be as close to perfection as any human being could possibly be (which, by the way, is not very close) and you could still be abused in the workplace.

There are many lawsuits involving unscrupulous employers that use bullying for strategic purposes. I have written elsewhere about encountering, in the course of my legal practice, young blue collar workers who were viciously bullied after they demanded legal wages and overtime pay. There are countless lawsuits involving employers who discharged employees for illegal reasons, such as to avoid paying unemployment benefits or workers compensation. The leading complaint filed with the U.S. Equal Employment Opportunity Commission involves retaliation by employers against employees who complain of illegal discrimination. Even a bona fide "bad" employee who deserves to be fired should be treated respectfully, with basic fairness and due process.

Bullies often select targets for reasons that have more to do with the bully than the target. Often targets are bullied because they are competent and popular. They pose a threat to the bully. Possibly the bully is trying to achieve status at the expense of a target who lacks social skills and self-esteem. In some cases, a workplace bully has no empathy for others' feelings and actually enjoys a target's anguish. Abusers also select targets for illegal reasons, including discrimination on the basis of race, disability, gender, pregnancy, religion, or national origin.

Your behavior, of course, is not irrelevant. An employer can compile a legitimate record of infractions and violations of company rules and regulations to justify your dismissal. For whatever reason, some employees are simply not suited for the job the employer hired them to do. However, a boss or employer is not entitled to drive workers out of the workplace by subjecting them to humiliating treatment, unfair criticism, lies, sabotage, harassment, ridicule, thwarting their ability to do their job, isolating them, overwhelming them with work, micro-managing them to the point of harassment, etc. These behaviors are not indicative of poor management or incivility. They constitute workplace bullying, which is a widely-recognized form of workplace *violence*.

Every worker has a legal right under the U.S. Occupational Safety and Health Act to work in a safe workplace. Overwhelming research shows that workers who are bullied suffer from a wide array of short-term and long term physical and mental injuries. These range from depression, anxiety and insomnia, to chronic health conditions, such as cardiovascular disease.

Slow on the Uptake?

There is no point in blaming yourself for failing to recognize that you were being bullied sooner. Many times targets don't recognize what is happening to them for weeks or months. By the time they do figure it out, the bully may have done serious damage to the target's work record and reputation. Bullying is irrational and unpredictable. It involves a pattern of behavior that unfolds through time. And abuse can easily be masked by the bully's supervisory authority.

Targets of bullying often go through predictable and time-consuming stages, which include denial and aversion, anger and resistance, acceptance and an attempt (usually futile) to bargain with management to save the target's job.

It is certainly possible that you are not entirely without blame for your workplace difficulties. Maybe you did something to undermine the goodwill of your supervisor. But no one deserved to be bullied.

Whatever you may have done, your boss has no right to abuse and harass you. Your employer has a legal responsibility to provide all workers with a safe workplace.

A target of workplace bullying is never at fault for the abusive behavior of a manager and/or the employer. And an employer that tolerates bullying is essentially forcing a target to quit because no target can withstand bullying forever. This is a form of constructive dismissal. If an employer wants to fire an employee, the employer should create a truthful record showing "cause" for termination so that it can defend its action if necessary in a subsequent unemployment hearing or court case.

Be Mindful

Many targets of workplace abuse find themselves engaged in a negative internal monologue. "Why am I so stupid?" "Why do I screw up everything I try to do?" They fail to acknowledge the reality of abuse. It is important to be mindful of your feelings so that you don't slip into self-loathing and blame.

Zen theory holds that what we think shapes how we perceive our reality. According to an ancient Buddhist verse:

> Watch your thoughts, for they become words.
>
> Watch your words, for they become actions.
>
> Watch your actions, for they become habits.
>
> Watch your habits, for they become character.
>
> Watch your character, for it becomes your destiny.

If you find yourself criticizing yourself for perceived flaws and failings, step back and ask yourself the following question: Would you demonstrate the same harshness toward a co-worker who is going through the kind of hostility and abuse that you are suffering at work?

Kristen Neff, PhD, author of *Self-Compassion: Stop Beating Yourself Up and Leave Insecurity Behind* (2015), argues that many of us are too quick to blame ourselves for not being good enough and for achieving less than perfection. She writes that exercising self compassion is a powerful way to achieve emotional well-being and contentment, while fostering happiness and optimism. According to Dr. Neff, self compassion has three basic components:

1) Extending kindness and understanding to oneself rather than harsh self-criticism and judgment;

2) Seeing one's experiences as part of the larger human experience rather than as separating and isolating; and

3) Holding one's painful thoughts and feelings in balanced awareness rather than over-identifying with them.

Neff writes that people instinctually dwell and ruminate on negative thoughts, rather than positive thoughts, as a self-protection mechanism. Self compassion, she says, is a "major protective factor" in warding off anxiety and depression.

Perspective

The Buddha taught that human suffering results from the inherent impermanency of human existence (the cycle of birth, aging, sickness and death). It is clinging to attachment and craving that *causes* suffering, not what is occurring in the outside world. For example, the fact that one ages is not painful per se. What is painful is when older people devalue themselves because they are no longer young and vital.

A job is an attachment. If you weren't attached to your job, it wouldn't matter to you if you lost it. Even if you don't care for your employer, you probably do care about your paycheck and financial security. It is not surprising that workers suffer when they face the possibility of unfair termination or being forced out of their job. Most workers also crave appropriate recognition and appreciation for their hard work. They suffer when they are denied credit or are unfairly criticized. It stands to reason that targets minimize their suffering when they minimize their attachment to a job and their craving for reward and recognition.

This doesn't mean that targets should sit by and do nothing while an abuser drives them out of the workplace. Acceptance refers not to accepting abuse but to recognize on a personal level that you are not your job or your cravings. And if you lose your job and your reputation, you will survive.

Many people treat the impermanency of the human condition like a shadow in a graveyard. We catch a glimpse of life's inherent unpredictability, quicken our step and try to ignore it. We work feverishly to build a dependable and comfortable existence and then we are surprised and devastated when things begin to fall apart.

Workers lose their jobs every day because of economic fluctuations that result in lay-offs when employers relocate to save labor costs to other states or foreign countries. New technology eliminates good jobs and even good professions. A change in management can mean dislocation for long-time, established workers. Workers reach a point where they can no longer do their jobs because of age, sickness or injury. The vast majority of dislocated workers survive. They find new jobs, buy new cars, get new houses, etc. It may not be easy but you will survive regardless of what happens to your job.

It makes little sense in the context of workplace abuse to be angry and disappointed when you are denied appropriate recognition for your skills, experience and hard work. Your emotional reaction won't change anything and may actually reward a bully who enjoys seeing your distress. It makes more sense to focus on the goal of developing a reasonable and appropriate response to the problem of bullying and abuse.

With acceptance comes clarity. By seeing the abuse for what it is, you will free yourself to respond effectively on a professional level to the abuse. Your response can be dispassionate and reasonable. You can, for example, turn your attention to gathering evidence so you can file a formal complaint pursuant to the company's internal complaint process.

The following self-compassion meditation can help you regain a sense of equanimity and help you treat yourself with the same kindness and compassion that you would extend to others in a similar situation.

I. Guided Self Compassion Medication

1) Sit erect on a chair or cushion.

2) Place your tongue on the roof of your mouth.

3) Cast your eyes downward.

4) Take three or four deep breaths. Allow your tension to slip away.

5) Gently place your hands on your heart, one over the other. Focus on the warm pulsing flow of blood through your heart. Feel your chest expand and contract. Your heart is the engine that makes your body run. Be thankful if you have a healthy heart. Many people suffer because they do not. Your health is more important than any transitory workplace problem.

6) Gather your attention to your body. Do your muscles feel tense? Is your stomach upset? Do you have a headache? Breathe in deeply and slowly exhale. Try to relax and get comfortable.

7) Direct your awareness to your emotions. How do you feel at this moment? Are you going through a difficult time? Do you recognize signs of suffering within yourself? Do you feel anxiety? Anger? Fear? Self pity? Unhappiness?

8) Now think about your feelings toward yourself. Are you angry or disappointed at yourself? Do you blame yourself for some failure or lapse of judgment? Do you feel unworthy or inferior? Recognize that all human beings make mistakes and no one is perfect. This is the human condition.

9) Think of a time when you noticed that a friend or loved one was suffering. Did your heart go out to your friend? Did you offer unconditional love and support? Did you sympathize with your friend's plight? Did you show kindness and compassion? What did you say or do to make your friend feel loved and supported?

10) Imagine that you are your own best friend. Recognize your suffering and let your heart go out

to yourself. All human beings have frailties as well as strengths. When we achieve less than perfection, we suffer. Show the same compassion for yourself that you would show to a friend or loved one. Comfort yourself with words and thoughts of loving kindness.

11) Repeat to yourself the following:

Let me be kind to myself.

Let me accept my human frailties.

Let me be strong in this difficult time.

Let me be free from suffering.

Let me be safe.

Let me live in peace.

12) Focus your awareness upon your heart center. All human beings depend upon this fragile organ to live. We are all both frail and strong. You have strength and weaknesses. And like every other

human being you are entitled to be treated with love and kindness.

13) With your hands over your heard, focus your awareness on your heart beating. Is your heart beating quickly or slowly. Notice but don't try to change anything.

14) Visualize a time when someone demonstrated loving kindness to you. Can you remember how it made you feel? Do you recall the feeling of being safe and cared for?

15) Repeat the following to yourself:

Let me be kind to myself.

Let me accept my human frailties.

Let me be strong in this difficult time.

Let me be free from suffering.

Let me be safe.

Let me live in peace.

16) Focus your awareness upon your beating heart. It is a sign of your vulnerability as an imperfect human being. You are no different from every other human being. We all have strength and weaknesses. You - like every other human being - are worthy of love and kindness.

17) If your mind wanders, don't worry. Simply return to your hand, and your heartbeat.

18) Now take your hands off your heart, opening your heart to the world. Repeat the following to yourself:

Let us all be kind to ourselves

Let us all accept our human frailties.

Let us be strong in difficult times.

Let us all be free from pain and suffering.

Let us all feel safe.

Let we all learn to live in peace together.

* This meditation was inspired by the groundbreaking research on self-compassion by Kristen Neff, PhD, a professor at the University of Texas, Austin.

II. THE FIVE YEAR OLD CHILD WITHIN

Zen Master and poet Thich Nhat Hanh said that all of us still have within us the five-year-old girl or boy that we were in our childhood.

Nhat Hanh notes that a young child is a precious treasure but also is vulnerable, gets hurt deeply and suffers terribly. He says the child within "is still alive and may be deeply wounded and neglected. He warns that the "wounded child" within may be causing you to suffer despair and pessimism.

If you smile at the little child within, Nhat Hanh says, you can heal the wounded child, develop self-compassion for yourself and improve the quality of happiness in your life. Nhat Hanh said this exercise also can help you avoid transmitting the trauma of your "wounded child" to others, such as your children and partners.

Nhat Hanh says this exercise is also useful to develop compassion for others. He suggests you

185

envision people who have been troublesome or unkind to you by seeing them as the five-year-old child they once were so that you can develop compassion toward them.

Nhat Hanh suggests developing self-compassion by meditating upon a picture of yourself (or the subject of your meditation) at the age of five.

Nhat Hanh was forcibly exiled from his native country of Vietnam more than 40 years ago. Civil rights leader Martin Luther King nominated Hanh for a Nobel Peace Prize in 1967.

III. SELF-KINDNESS PRAYERS & MEDITATIONS

First Be Kind to Yourself

First, let me be kind to myself.
Let me feel safe,
like a baby in the light of a parent's love.

I will be loving and kind to myself.
I am worthy of love and kindness.

Let me be happy with myself just as I am.
Like all human beings, I am frail.
Give me the compassion to accept my imperfections.

I will be loving and kind to myself.
I am worthy of love and kindness.

Give me the strength to endure
the cruelty and disrespect of others
by showing loving kindness toward myself.

I will be loving and kind to myself
for I am worthy of love and kindness.

Let me emerge from this dark time
with my spirit intact and
new compassion for myself and others.

————

To Those Who Suffer

Lift up the hearts of those who toil

in an abusive workplace,

tormented and unappreciated.

Protect them from the violence of oppressive
power.

Let us all be like the lotus flower

that shoots up through the muddy depths

until it breaks through

the surface of a still pond

pure and exquisite.

———

IV. REFLECTIONS BY THE BUDDHA

Thoughts

All that we are is the result of what we have thought:
it is founded on our thoughts,
it is made up of our thoughts.

If a man speaks or acts
with an evil thought, pain follows him,
as the wheel follows the foot of
the ox that draws the carriage.

All that we are is the result of what we have thought:
it is founded on our thoughts,
it is made up of our thoughts.

If a man speaks or acts with a pure thought,
happiness follows him,
like a shadow that never leaves him.

"He abused me, he beat me, he defeated me, he robbed me,"- in those who harbor such thoughts hatred will never cease.

189

"He abused me, he beat me, he defeated me, he robbed me."- in those who do not harbor such thoughts hatred will cease.

For hatred does not cease by hatred at any time: hatred ceases by love, this is an old rule.

The world does not know that we must all come to an end here - but those who know it, their quarrels cease at once.

Self

Let each man direct himself first to what is proper, then let him teach others; thus a wise man will not suffer.

If a man make himself as he teaches others to be, then, being himself well subdued, he may subdue (others); one's own self is indeed difficult to subdue...

The evil done by oneself, self-begotten, self-bred, crushes the foolish, as a diamond breaks a precious stone.

He whose wickedness is very great brings himself down to that state where his enemy wishes him to be, as a creeper does with the tree which it surrounds.

Bad deeds, and deeds hurtful to ourselves, are easy to do; what is beneficial and good, that is very difficult to do.

By oneself the evil is done, by oneself one suffers; by oneself evil is left undone, by oneself one is purified.

Purity and impurity belong to oneself, no one can purify another.

————

Happiness

Let us live happily then,

not hating those who hate us!

Among men who hate us let us dwell free from hatred!

Let us live happily then,

free from ailments among the ailing!

Among men who are ailing let us dwell free from ailments!

Let us live happily then,

free from greed among the greedy!

Among men who are greedy let us dwell free from greed!

Let us live happily then,

though we call nothing our own!

We shall be like the bright gods, feeding on happiness!

Victory breeds hatred, for the conquered is unhappy.

He who has given up both victory and defeat,
he, the contented, is happy.

Anger

Let a man leave anger, let him forsake pride, let him overcome all bondage!

No sufferings befall the man who is not attached to name and form, and who calls nothing his own.

He who holds back rising anger like a rolling chariot, him I call a real driver; other people are but holding the reins.

Let a man overcome anger by love, let him overcome evil by good; let him overcome the greedy by liberality, the liar by truth!

Speak the truth, do not yield to anger; give, if thou art asked for little; by these three steps thou wilt go near the gods.

* The Project Gutenberg EBook of The Dhammapada, by Unknown. Translator: F. Max Muller, available at http://www.gutenberg.org/files/2017/2017-h/2017-h.htm.

Flowers

A bee collects pollen and then leaves, never harming the flower.

Neither the color nor the fragrance are diminished in any way.

In this way, I travel through life.

Instead of focusing on the faults of others,

The wrongs they have done, the good they have failed to do,

I look clearly at my own acts,

What I do, and what I leave undone.

Like a beautiful and colorful blossom that has no scent

Are words of wisdom spoken by one who does not practice them?

Like a beautiful blossom with a rich, sweet scent.

Are words of wisdom spoken by one who puts them into practice?

Many different kinds of garlands can be made

with the same heap of flowers.

Many different kinds of good deeds

can be done between my birth and death in this world.

The scents of flowers cannot blow against the wind.

Neither can the perfumes of jasmine, sandalwood, or clove.

but the fragrance of virtue radiates in every direction.

Jasmine, sandalwood, lotus, and clove:

The fragrance of virtue far surpasses all of these.

The fragrances of lavish perfumes grow faint

but the fragrance of virtue stays strong.

It wafts up even to the heavens

The Dhammapada: A Practitioner's Translation, Wikisource "The Free Library" Religious Texts, http://www.freemedialibrary.com/index.php/The_Dhamm apada:_A_Practitioner%27s_Translation

Chapter 11

COMPASSION FOR YOUR ENEMY

"Fools, their wisdom weak, are their own enemies as they go through life, doing evil that bears bitter fruit." - *the Buddha*

Why would anyone feel compassion toward an abusive supervisor?

Zen does not ask people to submit to abuse and disrespect. Indeed, that is not advisable. Research shows that living with constant anger, hatred and fear is unhealthy. It can ravage an individual's immune system and lead to potentially severe illness and disease. Negative emotions drive people to abuse alcohol and drugs and leads to the disintegration of families. Under Zen theory, individuals benefit, mentally and physically, from fostering and maintaining a sense of calm and compassion toward everyone, including toward those who least deserve it. Zen theory holds that happiness comes from empathizing with others and from seeing that their wellbeing and suffering as just as important as your own.

The point is not to establish a friendship. Targets should continue to pursue whatever avenues are available and necessary to stop the abuse, even if that means having the bully unceremoniously fired. Targets have a responsibility to protect themselves and others from abuse. But targets can make their lives easier until there is a resolution to the problem by choosing how to respond to abuse. They cannot control an abusive boss or co-worker but they can respond with kindness and compassion, rather than hate and anger.

There is another reason to be kind and compassionate to an abusive supervisor that may counter-intuitive. Abusers typically show an enthusiastic and solicitous face to management while treating their subordinates with cruelty and contempt.

They may achieve great success and all of the accoutrements that accompany success – a big office, high paycheck recognition, etc. But all may not be as it appears on the outside. Traditional Buddhist theory holds that abusers suffer because of their own bad acts.

Under Zen theory, people who inflict pain and hardship on others invite suffering upon themselves.

The Buddha repeatedly stressed that people reap what they sow. In other words, if you abuse others, you will not find inner peace yourself and you may well be inviting harm upon yourself.

The suffering of abusers not only prevents them from attaining happiness in this life but also in the next life. Buddhists believe that people are reborn after they die in a state that is higher or lower depending upon their actions in this life. This belief incorporates the concept of transmigration –the effects of our good and bad actions extend from our former lives to the present and from our present lives to our future lives. People

199

who act badly in this life are seen as being en-route to
their grave in dire straits.

*"Don't let greed and unrighteousness oppress
you with long-term pain," advised the Buddha.*

Why should you care if your abuser is suffering?
There is a Buddhist story that is similar to the biblical
story of the Good Samaritan. In the Buddhist story an
old man lay gravely ill on a path that is located between
two villages. He has no food or medicine and no way to
get assistance from a nurse or doctor. Buddhists are
asked whether they would extend kindness and
compassion to this man or turn their back on him and
walk away. Clearly the expectation is that a good
Buddhist would help the ill man. Similarly, in the Good
Samaritan story, a passer-by is lauded for helping a man
who was beaten by thieves and lay by the side of the
road. A workplace bully or abuser is like the gravely ill
man lying on the highway. His or her suffering is
spiritual and has dire consequences in this life that will
continue into the next life.

Finally, the Buddha said the act of focusing obsessively on the harm done to you by another harms you. The Buddha said that when individuals repeatedly think about and complain about the way they are being treated, they become self-centered. This is an impediment to *their* search for happiness. The Buddha urged his followers to rid themselves of "defilements" like selfishness, envy, egotism, anger, and hate so they can find inner peace.

Understandably, it is a challenge for targets to be kind and compassionate to someone who is intent upon harming them. Geshe Lobsang Tenzin, director of the Emory University-Tibet Partnership, says targets can develop compassion for people who are evil or who have harmed them by looking for signs of common aspirations and shared humanity. It might help you develop compassion for your enemy by recognizing that you share common goals. Doesn't everyone want to be happy, fulfilled, free and loved? According to the Dali Lama, all human beings are "100 percent" the same "mentally, emotionally, physically... No matter what appearance. We all have the desire to achieve a happy life."

Zen theory holds that through meditation, we can find innate compassion and wisdom, which we can use to benefit ourselves and all beings. What follows are meditations and prayers designed to help targets address the suffering they have experienced from an abusive supervisor through loving kindness and compassion.

I. COMPASSION FOR YOUR ENEMY

This meditation involves several steps that are designed to open your heart, as well as the heart of your enemy.

1) *See* Chapter 8, Preliminary Steps.

2) Think of someone you love, such as a parent, partner, child or even a dog or cat. It is easy to generate feelings of compassion for loved ones who are suffering and need help. Visualize your loved one in your mind. Notice how you feel when you think of this loved one. Does thinking about this person make your feel warm and happy? Let your attention rest there for a moment.

3) *Inhale.* Imagine your loved one's suffering as a thick, heavy black smoke. As you inhale, draw all of the smoke into your own body and take it away from your loved one.

4) *Exhale.* Visualize your own happiness and well being as a ray of brilliant white, cooling light. As

you exhale send a ray of light to your loved one to relieve your loved one of all pain and suffering. Wish your loved one freedom from stress, fear and suffering.

5) Now expand your visualization to include someone who is dear to you, like a friend or neighbor.

6) Repeat the steps above, this time on behalf of your friend.

7) Wish that your friend experience freedom from fear and suffering and joy as well as good health and a sense of over-all well-being.

8) Finally, expand your visualization to include someone whom you dislike – your abusive supervisor or the co-workers who are making your work life miserable.

9) Repeat the steps above, this time on behalf of your enemy. Wish that your enemy experience an end to suffering and the grace of good health. Then repeat the following:

May my enemy be filled with loving-kindness.

May my enemy be well.

May my enemy be peaceful and at ease.

May my enemy be happy.

10) Finally, open your heart fully to the universe.

11) Wish that everyone everywhere experiences an end to suffering, as well as peace, happiness and good health.

II. MEDITATION FOR A WORKPLACE BULLY

1) Visualize the manager or supervisor who is subjecting you to abusive behaviors at work.

2) Think about the suffering of this person. He or she has conflicts with loved ones, insecurities and failures and has experienced illness and loss. Can you think of a situation at the workplace where you saw this person suffer?

3) Focus on your heart center. What sensations do you feel? Warmth... Openness... Understanding... Compassion?

4) Again, visualize this person as you breathe in and out.

5) As you exhale, imagine that you are extending a gentle and restoring light from your heart to his or hers, and that the light eases this person's suffering.

6) As you inhale, make a genuine and sincere wish that this person be freed from suffering. Make this wish

as strong as it would be if you were wishing to ease your own suffering or that of a loved one.

7) As you think of this person, silently recite:

May you be free from suffering.

May you have joy and happiness.

If you find it hard to genuinely desire to relieve your enemy's suffering, try to visualize a positive interaction with this person. Did you ever get along? Share a laugh? Work well together?

8) Continue to silently recite:

May you be free from suffering.

May you have joy and happiness.

9) Return to your heart center. Do you feel warmth? Openness? Do you feel tightness in your chest? Did you really want to take away this person's suffering? If not, don't worry. Just try again tomorrow.

* Inspired by a study by Helen Weng, et.al. Changing your Brain and Generosity Through Compassion

Meditation Training, Center for Investigating Healthy Minds, University of Wisconsin. At http://www.investigatinghealthyminds.org/cihmProjMeditation.html.

III. THERAVADA LOVING KINDNESS PRAYER

Theravada is the oldest surviving branch of Buddhism. The word is derived from the Sanskrit and means "the Teaching of the Elders". Loving-kindness prayer meditations are recited daily at Theravada Buddhist temples.

The following loving-kindness prayer meditation extends loving-kindness in seven different directions: to ourselves, parents, teachers, relatives, friends, enemies, and then all beings in the universe.

May I be well, happy, and peaceful.

May no harm come to me.

May no difficulties come to me.

May no problems come to me.

May I have patience, courage, understanding, and determination to meet and overcome inevitable difficulties, problems, and failures in life.

May my parents (and/or children) be well, happy, and peaceful.

May no harm come to them.

May no difficulties come to them.

May no problems come to them.

May they have patience, courage, understanding, and determination to meet and overcome inevitable difficulties, problems, and failures in life.

May my teachers be well, happy, and peaceful.

May no harm come to them.

May no difficulties come to them.

May no problems come to them.

May they have patience, courage, understanding, and determination to meet and overcome inevitable difficulties, problems, and failures in life.

May my friends be well, happy, and peaceful.

May no harm come to them.

May no difficulties come to them.

May no problems come to them.

May they have patience, courage, understanding, and determination to meet and overcome inevitable difficulties, problems, and failures in life.

May my enemies be well, happy, and peaceful.

May no harm come to them.

May no difficulties come to them.

May no problems come to them.

May they have patience, courage, understanding, and determination to meet and overcome inevitable difficulties, problems, and failures in life.

May all beings in the universe be well, happy, and peaceful.

May no harm come to them.

May no difficulties come to them.

May no problems come to them.

May they have patience, courage, understanding, and determination to meet and overcome inevitable difficulties, problems, and failures in life..

The above prayer/meditation is inspired by a lengthier Loving Kindness Prayer Meditation by Dr. Henepola Gunaratana Nayaka Thera, Buddhist Prayer: An Anthology, Jason Espada, editor. (2011). See http://www.abuddhistlibrary.com/Buddhism/B%20-%20Theravada/Metta/Meditation%20on%20Loving%20Kindness/II/Loving%20Kindness%20II.htm

IV. SELF-COMPASSION PRAYER-MEDITATION

Difference

On the outside

We are different.

We have different faiths,

Different histories,

Different politics,

Different emotions,

Different dreams.

But inside

We are the same.

Difference is an illusion

Like a mirage

Like the moon on the water.

May you find kindness and compassion

Before your journey ends.

Peace and Justice

In their hearts

In their dreams,

And in their lives

Those who hold firm to a vision of peace and justice toward others

Experience peace and justice.

Those who do not hold firm to a vision of peace and justice toward others

Condemn themselves

To suffer injustice and unhappiness.

Let every living being on the face of the earth

Experience the joy of peace and justice.

———————

V. REFLECTIONS BY THE BUDDHA

Evil

Let no man think lightly of evil, saying in his heart, It will not come nigh unto me.

Even by the falling of water-drops a water-pot is filled; the fool becomes full of evil, even if he gather it little by little.

Let no man think lightly of good, saying in his heart, It will not come nigh unto me.

Even by the falling of water-drops a water-pot is filled; the wise man becomes full of good, even if he gather it little by little.

———

215

Punishment

He who seeking his own happiness punishes or kills beings who also long for happiness, will not find happiness after death.

He who seeking his own happiness does not punish or kill beings who also long for happiness, will find happiness after death.

Do not speak harshly to anybody; those who are spoken to will answer thee in the same way.

Angry speech is painful, blows for blows will touch thee.

The Project Gutenberg EBook of The Dhammapada, by Unknown. Translator: F. Max Muller, available at http://www.gutenberg.org/files/2017/2017-h/2017-h.htm.

The Fool

Foolish people with poor understanding
Are their own worst enemies.

They plant the seeds of unethical acts
And when the plant grows to a tree, the fruit is
bitter.

When I do something but later regret it,
Weeping and mourning,
Then I should not have done it in the first place.

But when I do something
And look back on it with true gladness,
Then it was a good deed to have done.

An evil deed may seem, to a fool,
To be as sweet as honey,

But only because it has not yet ripened.
When it ripens, the fool comes to grief.

*The Dhammapada: A Practitioner's Translation,
Wikisource "The Free Library" Religious Texts,
http://www.freemedialibrary.com/index.php/The_Dhamm
apada:_A_Practitioner%27s_Translation

Chapter 12

ASSORTED MEDITATIONS

"Pain is certain, suffering is optional."
- the Buddha

There are many types of meditation. Just a few of them are included here. They were chosen because they are appropriate to most workplace settings.

I. Visualization

Visualize a simple concept that is reaffirming.

a. Solid Like a Mountain

Zen Master Thich Nhat Hanh, a poet and peace activist from Vietnam, developed a mindfulness meditation that could be helpful to people who are targets of workplace abuse. When you feel vulnerable,

Nhat Hanh says, picture yourself as being solid like a mountain.

He suggests that you sit comfortably in a chair and focus on your navel as a point of awareness because it is located in the most solid part of your body.

As you inhale say, "I see myself as a mountain."

As you exhale say, "I am solid."

Repeat each statement as time allows.

Nhat Hanh says you can eliminate verbiage as you go along and say, for example, only "mountain" and "solid."

Often, targets of workplace abuse feel vulnerable, like a leaf clinging to a tree branch on a windy day. Visualizing yourself as mountain may help you feel less vulnerable.

Nhat Hanh's meditation also follows a very flexible format. You can easily tailor this format to create a visual meditation that is meaningful to you.

Can you think of something that has a special meaning that you could incorporate into a visualization meditation?

b. *Resilient Like A Lifeboat*

Any meditation can be tailored to make it more meaningful. For example, instead of picturing a mountain, you can focus on a statue of Jesus or the Buddha. Or pick something significant in your own life.

At one time, I worked as a newspaper reporter and I covered the U.S. Coast Guard Academy in New London, CT. I became familiar with the fleet of water vessels used by the Coast Guard to patrol American waters. These vessels range from The Eagle, an elegant tall ship, to the tiny Motor Lifeboat, a remarkable aluminum boat that is used on rescue missions in severe weather.

The Motor Lifeboat is virtually unsinkable. A series of ballast compartments in the hull forces the boat to float upright. If the 47-foot long boat capsizes, it will return to an upright position within eight seconds and all equipment on the boat will be fully intact and operational.

The resiliency of this lifeboat allows a four-person crew to rescue people in what otherwise would be hopeless circumstances. In 1996, for example, a tug boat towing a large oil barge off the coast of Rhode Island exploded, throwing six crew members overboard in stormy seas. The Motor Lifeboat conquered 30-foot-high ocean swells and hurricane force winds to save all six lives. Here is a possible visualization meditation based upon the Motor Lifeboat:

Breathe deeply in through your nose. Exhale through your mouth.

Lower or close your eyes.

Scan your body for areas of tension. Relax tense muscles. Start with your eyebrows, shoulders, arms, legs, down to your feet.

With each breath, feel your tension lessen and fade away.

Imagine a sleek white boat cutting through ocean swells. This boat will not sink even if it capsizes. It will always return to an upright position within eight seconds, with all equipment intact and ready for use.

As you inhale, say, "I see myself as an unsinkable boat."

As you exhale, say, "I am resilient."

As you inhale, say, "I see myself as an unsinkable boat."

As you exhale, say, "I am resilient."

Repeat as time allows.

A meditation about an unsinkable boat would be appropriate for targets of workplace abuse. Many fear they will lose their jobs. In truth, if the worst happens and you do "capsize" - you are fired or forced to quit - you will right yourself. Many workers lose their jobs every day and, like the Motor Lifeboat, they end up in an upright position with all of their faculties intact. You will find a new and better job, hopefully with an employer that does not tolerate workplace abuse.

II. Walking Meditation

Instead of a "desk meditation," get up from your work station and do a "walking meditation." Or use the time between appointments or your lunch break to walk mindfully.

The Buddha is said to have walked 250 kilometers to Deer Park, Benares, from Bodyghaya, his place of enlightenment. Alone and barefoot, the Buddha walked in the searing heat of summer. He made the journey to preach his first sermon about the true cause of suffering to his former companions, the five ascetics. The ascetics planned to ignore him when he arrived but they were so taken by his majestic appearance that they prepared a place for him using their own tattered clothing.

A walking meditation is an exercise in mindfulness that focuses upon the breath and each footfall or step.

When workers normally walk during their workday, their pace is often more akin to a gallop than a walk because of awareness of time constraints. During a meditative walk, the pace should be slower than normal. The idea is to enjoy your walk, while remaining mindful.

At a Zen meditation center, meditators might walk in a straight line up and down a row or in a circle. Ideally, you would engage in a walking meditation in a beautiful natural area where you could enjoy earth's beauty. If that is not available to you, adapt your walking meditation to the environment that is available. If you work at a retail mall, for example, walk around the mall. You can engage in a walking meditation alone or with a co-worker or friend.

Here's what Beat Generation writer Jack Kerouac wrote about walking meditation in his 1958 book, *The Dharma Bums*:

"Try the meditation of the trail, just walk along looking at the trail at your feet and don't look about and just fall into a trance as the ground zips by. Trails are like that: you're floating along in a Shakespearean Arden paradise and expect to see nymphs and fluteboys, then suddenly you're struggling in a hot broiling sun of hell in dust and nettles and poison oak... just like life."

III. Sound Meditation

There are many variants of sound meditation. One variant is to produce a sound, such as the sacred mantra "OM," by singing it or repeating it again and again until you experience a transcendent state. This is probably not practical in a busy office setting. But another way to use sound in a meditation practice is just to listen.

Some people find it difficult to meditate in an office because it is noisy. Every tick of a clock sounds like the gong of a bell tower. You can don a pair of noise cancelling earphones or you can embrace the sound and use it as part of your meditation practice.

Another meditation variation is to listen to music when you meditate. Don headphones or earplugs or simply enjoy the generic music piped by your employer through the workplace. Hear each note of music and the silence in between, all without judgment. Coordinate your breath with the beat of the music.

CONCLUSION

> "Let us rise up and be thankful, for if we didn't learn a lot at least we learned a little, and if we didn't learn a little, at least we didn't get sick, and if we got sick, at least we didn't die; so, let us all be thankful." – *the Buddha*

One of the Buddha's most revolutionary teachings was that people don't have to wait around for salvation. The Buddha taught that it is the responsibility of each individual - and it is within each individual's power - to save themselves. In fact, he stressed that no one else can do it for them.

This is a particularly fitting message for targets of workplace abuse in the United States because the U.S. lags far behind other industrialized countries in protecting American workers from workplace bullying. For more than a decade, corporate interests have successfully stymied efforts to pass state laws to protect American workers from bullying. On top of that, the

U.S. Supreme Court presently is the most "anti-worker" court since World War II. The Court seems intent on invalidating rather than safeguarding worker protections. Meanwhile, Republicans and Democrats in the U.S. Congress have ignored the suffering of the American worker, while raking in campaign contributions from the aforesaid corporate interests.

The bottom line is that targets of workplace bullying who do not belong to a union or who lack the protection of a written contract– the vast majority of all workers- are pretty much on their own. No one else is coming to save the day. If you don't safeguard your own health and "save" your job, the chances are that no one else will.

As noted in prior chapters, there are many things that targets can and should do to help themselves:

1) First targets must recognize if they are being bullied and abused by a boss or manager in the workplace. If they even suspect this, they should start keeping a journal and begin recording in detail each instance

of bullying or abuse. At some point, a pattern may emerge. This journal could serve as evidence if you receive a negative evaluation, are threatened with termination or fired. The journal also is potentially key evidence in an unemployment compensation appeal or lawsuit.

2) Targets must recognize that they are suffering emotionally and perhaps physically because they are being bullied and abused. Often targets are in denial or too busy trying to fix the problem to see that they are being steadily worn down, as if they were battling a chronic sinus condition or vitamin deficiency. They often make things worse for themselves by blaming themselves for mistakes or for not being perfect. This represents a fundamental misunderstanding about workplace abuse. It's never the target's fault that s/he is being harassed, lied to, sabotaged, given too much work, held to unattainable deadlines. micromanaged, ignored, embarrassed, ridiculed, etc. It's the employer's

responsibility to provide workers with a safe workplace, free from bullying and abuse.

3) Targets should embrace the Zen theory of mindfulness and regularly meditate (even if it is only for short periods) to seek clarity about their situation and to protect themselves from corrosive anxiety and stress. Overwhelming research shows that meditation relieves stress and anxiety.

4) Invoke your employer's complaint system even if it does not seem particularly promising. By complaining, targets put the employer on notice that they are being bullied. Notice can be critical if the target eventually files a lawsuit. If an employer fails to halt abuse after being made aware of it, the employer faces greater liability if the abuse continues. Alternatively, if you don't notify your employer that you are suffering abuse, you may forfeit the ability to make your employer pay damages to compensate you for your suffering in future litigation.

5) If you complain and the company does nothing, consider talking to an employment attorney who represents workers (not employers) about what, if any, legal avenues are open to you. A consultation should be free or inexpensive. In many communities, the local bar association provides opportunities to consult with an attorney at a government building or library, once a month.

6) Considering working with a therapist. For one thing, it's helpful to have someone to talk to about the problem. But importantly, if you are feeling stressed out, the visits to the therapist are evidence of your fragile emotional state. Also, you may qualify for unpaid leave under the Family and Medical Leave Act. Your employer may require a doctor's certification supporting your request for unpaid leave.

Although there are clear benefits to lodging a bullying complaint, research shows the strategy adopted by most targets is to avoid contact with an abusive supervisor. This avoidance increases the target's stress.

In Zen theory (and my experience) inaction rarely is a good option for targets of workplace abuse. The problem usually does not go away until the target goes away. According to the Workplace Bullying Institute, 64 percent of targets quit or are fired and 13 percent transfer to a different job. Meanwhile, targets become more and more worn down by exposure to debilitating hostility, which makes it increasingly difficult to respond effectively to abuse. And delay gives the boss more time to sabotage the target with poor evaluations and warnings.

If a target does file a complaint and the employer fails to take corrective action is taken, several legal theories may come into play.

Title VII of the Civil Rights Act of 1964 protects workers on the basis of race, gender, religion, color and national origin. If a bullied worker has grounds to link bullying to illegal discrimination, the target can file a lawsuit. Other laws protect workers from discrimination on the basis of age and disability. Workers who are not protected by civil rights laws may be able to shoehorn their case into another legal theory, such as a contract or personal injury action, including Intentional Infliction of Emotional Distress.

The reality is that the vast majority of targets of workplace abuse never get justice in the American legal system. First, there is no law specifically addressing workplace bullying. Some employers either don't care about their workers' welfare or confuse bullying with tough management. Some employers actually use bullying strategically to avoid a legal duty, such as paying workers' compensation. Secondly most workers can't afford justice. Few middle class workers and even fewer poor workers have the resources to pay an attorney's retainer, never mind the others costs of a lawsuit. Lastly, workers who can afford to access the federal court system will encounter judges with lifetime tenure who are not sympathetic to workers struggling with abuse. Research shows that federal judges dismiss employment discrimination cases at a disproportionately higher rate than other types of cases.

There is a story that shortly after the Buddha's enlightenment, he passed a stranger on the road. The man was so struck by the Buddha's calm radiance that he asked him, "Are you a god?"

"No. I am not." replied the Buddha.

"What are you then?" the man asked.

"I am awake." said the Buddha.

In a sense, Zen theory and meditation awaken targets of bullying and abuse to the reality of their situation. This allows targets to identify the problem and to respond effectively. It takes time to gather evidence to file a complaint demonstrating a pattern of abuse. Meditation is a tool that allows targets to better handle debilitating anxiety and fear, thus buying time to remain in a hostile workplace until a complaint is resolved.

Most importantly, Zen empowers targets who might otherwise respond impulsively and emotionally to be reflective and respond calmly and reasonably. In my law practice, I have seen cases where targets of bullying effectively shot themselves in the foot by impulsively and inappropriately responding to bullying tactics.

The Buddha said the "real goal is liberation or absolute freedom from bondage." He was talking about freedom from suffering caused by the human condition and its endless cycle of birth and death. In the context of a difficult workplace, however, Zen offers targets freedom from another kind of bondage - the tyranny of an abusive boss or employer.

Be proactive.

Take responsibility.

Save your sanity and your job.

237

SELECTED REFERENCES

Books

Ambedkar, Dr. B.R., *The Buddha and his Dhamma* (1957).

Bhikkhu, Buddhadasa, *Buddha-Dharma for Students: Answers to questions a non-Buddhist is likely to ask about the fundamentals of Buddhism* (1988).

Bhodi, Bhikkhu, *In the Buddha's Words* (2005).

Genner, Christopher K. *The Mindful Path to Self-Compassion: Freeing Yourself from Destructive Thoughts and Emotions* (2009).

Hahn, Thich Nhat, *The Miracle of Mindfulness; An Introduction to the Practice of* Meditation (1976).

Huang-Po, *The Zen Teaching of Huang-Po: On the Transmission of Mind*, Translated by John Eaton Calthorpe Blofeld (1994).

Kaye, Les, *Zen at Work* (1996).

Lama, Dalai & Howard C. Cutler, M.D., *The Art of Happiness at Work*, (2003).

Muller, F. Max, et al., *Studies in Buddhism* (1988).

Metcalf, F. & Gallagher, *What Would Buddha Do at Work?* (1996).

Neff, Kristen, PhD, *Self-Compassion: Stop Beating Yourself Up and Leave Insecurity Behind (2011)*.

Smith, Jean, *The Beginner's Guide to Zen Buddhism* (2000).

Suzuki, Daisetz T., *Zen Buddhism* (1956), William Barrett Ed.

There, Nayanaponika, *The Heart of Buddhist Meditation* (1962).

Wallace, Allan B. *Tibetan Buddhism From the Ground Up: A Practical Approach for a Modern Life* (1996).

Selected References

Watts, Alan, *The Way of Zen* (1957).

Articles

Ajahn Sucitto, *Mindfulness Of Mind*, Audio Talk, Chithurst Buddhist Monastery, West Sussex, England. Downloaded on 7/16/2013 at http://www.cittaviveka.org/. Mr. Sucitto is a Buddhist monk and the abbot of Chithurst Buddhist Monastery.

Hölzel, B.K., *et. al, Stress reduction correlates with structural changes in the amygdale.* Social Cognitive and Affective Neuroscience, (2009).

Hölzel, B.K, et. al, *.Mindfulness practice leads to increases in regional brain gray matter density,* Psychiatry Research – Neuroimaging, (January 2011).

Rock, David, *The Neuroscience of Mindfulness,* Psychology Today (Oct. 2009), downloaded on 7/15/13 from http://www.psychologytoday.com/blog/your-brain-work/200910/the-neuroscience-mindfulness.

Other

Compassion Meditation: Mapping Current Research and Charting Future Directions, Emory University (10/18/2010). See:
Part One: http://www.youtube.com/watch?v=739od6PVGgs
Part Two:
http://www.youtube.com/watch?v=tVes5vao2a8

ABOUT THE AUTHOR

Patricia G. Barnes is a licensed attorney and a former judge who has written several books on workplace bullying, employment discrimination and abuse.

She wrote the best-selling legal guide to workplace bullying and abuse, *Surviving Bullies, Queen Bees & Psychopaths in the Workplace* (2012). She is also the author of *Overcoming Age Discrimination in Employment: An Essential Guide for Workers, Advocates & Employers* (2016) and *Betrayed: The Legalization of Age Discrimination in the Workplace* (2014).

She writes a syndicated legal blog entitled Abuser Goes to Work at abusergoestowork.com. She also counsels workers and employers about how to deal with the problems of employment discrimination, workplace bullying and abuse.

Her other books include *CQ's Desk Reference on American Criminal Justice* (2000) and *CQ's Desk Reference on American Courts* (1999).